taekyon

The Korean Martial Art

An Anthology of Articles from
the *Journal of Asian Martial Arts*
Compiled by Michael A. DeMarco, M.A.

Disclaimer
Please note that the authors and publisher of this book are not responsible in any manner whatsoever for any injury that may result from practicing the techniques and/or following the instructions given within. Since the physical activities described herein may be too strenuous in nature for some readers to engage in safely, it is essential that a physician be consulted prior to training.

All Rights Reserved
No part of this publication, including illustrations, may be reproduced or utilized in any form or by any means, electronic or mechanical, including photocopying, recording, or by any information storage and retrieval system (beyond that copying permitted by sections 107 and 108 of the US Copyright Law and except by reviewers for the public press), without written permission from Via Media Publishing Company.

Warning: Any unauthorized act in relation to a copyright work may result in both a civil claim for damages and criminal prosecution.

Copyright © 2016
by Via Media Publishing Company
941 Calle Mejia #822, Santa Fe, NM 87501 USA

All articles in this anthology were originally
published in the *Journal of Asian Martial Arts*.
Listed according to the table of contents for this anthology:

Henning, S. (200), Vol. 9 No. 1, pp. 8-15
Young, R. (1993), Vol. 2 No 2, pp. 44-69
Pieter, W. (1994), Vol. 3 No. 1, pp. 82-89
Yung, O. (1997), Vol. 6 No. 4, pp. 76-89

Book and cover design by
Via Media Publishing Company

Edited by
Michael A. DeMarco, M.A.

Cover illustration
Taekyon kicking practice.
Photograph courtesy of the Dahmul Culture Center.
Photography by Ko You-sun.

ISBN: 9781983765399

www.viamediapublishing.com

contents

iv **Preface**
by Michael DeMarco, M.A.

CHAPTERS

1 **Traditional Korean Martial Arts**
by Stanley E. Henning, M.A.

10 **The History and Development of Taekyon**
by Robert W. Young

39 **Notes on the Historical Development of Korean Martial Sports: An Addendum to Young's History and Development of Taekyon**
by Willy Pieter, Ph.D.

47 **The Elevation of Taekyon from Folk Game to Martial Art**
by Yung Ouyang, B.A.

61 **Index**

preface

When people discuss Korean martial arts, they rarely mention taekyon. They are usually totally unfamiliar with the name because there hasn't been much written about it. The four chapters in this anthology give an excellent overview of taekyon as a system noted for it's dance-like qualities and combative style, especially for leg techniques. Taekyon stands unique as it represents most closely to a pure Korean martial tradition.

Chapter one by Stanley Henning gives a detailed overview of martial arts in Korea. From the beginning, Korean martial arts were intertwined with those of China. Even the historical references to Korean martial arts are all in Chinese. The author concludes that traditional Korean martial arts are but a vague memory, with taekyon being the sole survivor.

In the next chapter, Robert Young skillfully presents what is known about taekyon. With over 150 years of verifiable history, taekyon is the most thoroughly documented of Korean martial arts. Its skills and techniques greatly differ from those of other modern Korean styles. It is the only plausible candidate for the descendant of ancient subak. This well-researched chapter includes theory and techniques and lineage chart.

Dr. Willy Pieter expands upon the historical development of Korean martial sports as presented by Young. There is an emphasis on the *hwarang* ("flower boy") and their presence in Korean culture and martial traditions in particular. The etymology of Korean martial systems are questioned.

The final chapter by Yung Ouyang offers a fuller picture of what taekyon represents as a moving art. Traditionally, taekyon was a game as well as a martial art, so many did not credit taekyon for its combative elements. It has largely been ignored by those interested in the fighting arts. It is gaining recognition as a legitimate heir to the traditional Korean martial arts, but is also undergoing influences from Japanese traditions and Western sports.

Taekyon deserves to be recognized for its uniqueness among the martial arts of Asia. This anthology will serve as solid reference for all interested in the Korean combative traditions, and especially taekyon for its aesthetic appeal as a form of dance and graceful yet powerful combative method.

Michael A. DeMarco, Publisher
Santa Fe, New Mexico
November 2016

chapter 1

Traditional Korean Martial Arts
by Stanley E. Henning, M.A.

From the beginning, Korean martial arts were intertwined with those of China. Even the historical references to Korean martial arts are all in Chinese, the literary language of the Korean elites over the centuries. The earliest archaeological evidence of Korean martial arts practices (not necessarily of pure Korean origin) is found in one of a group of tombs in northeast China, an area under the Koguryo Kingdom (37 BCE-668 CE), but colonized and under Chinese military control between 108 BCE and 313 CE (No, 1974: 140-41; Mizuno, 1972). The wall murals at this site include one scene which clearly depicts wrestling (*juedi* in Chinese and *kakjo* in Korean) and another with two protagonists rushing at each other which has been interpreted by some as depicting boxing (*shoubo* in Chinese and *subak* in Korean). Whether or not the latter scene actually depicts boxing as opposed to wrestling remains a matter of conjecture, but what is known is that, already by this time, Chinese martial arts had developed to a relatively high degree of sophistication with a clear distinction made between wrestling and boxing practices.

Under the first Qin Dynasty (221-210 BCE) emperor, wrestling was designated as the official military ceremonial activity and sport while, during the Former Han period (206 BCE-24 CE), boxing was categorized as one of several military skills, which even included a form of football, "...to practice hand and foot movements, facilitate use of weapons, and organize for victory in offense or defense" (Chen, 1977: 2961; Gu, 1987: 205). This game of football was also adopted by the Koreans during their Three Kingdoms period (57-668), which arose toward the end of the Chinese Former Han (No, 1974: 147-158).

In most popular Korean and English writings on the subject, the primary bit of evidence offered for the existence of a Korean form of boxing during the long period between the early cave murals and records on the Koryo period (well over 1000 years) is the presence of the stone guardian figures at the entrance to the Sokkuram Buddhist site dating to the Unified Silla period (mid-8th century). These guardians are in the style common to contemporary Tang China (618-907) on which they were most assuredly modeled. Even some reputable Korean sources refer to these figures as "wrestlers" rather than "boxers," but they are most commonly called "strong men" (*lishi* in Chinese or *ryuksa* in Korean) (Kim, 1978: 15-16; Ministry, 1956: 194-95). Some writers tend to read too much into the poses of these figures, which can be viewed as actual forms used in Chinese-style boxing, but which are primarily symbolic. The Chinese character for "fist" also meant "strength" (*quan* in Chinese, *kwon* in Korean), but did not refer to boxing in China until the Southern Song (1127-1279). There is no evidence that it was ever used to refer to boxing in Korea, until relatively recently, except in quoting Chinese sources in the *Illustrated Encyclopedia of Martial Arts Manuals* (*Muye Dobo Tongji*, 1790). Nevertheless, boxing in the form of subak almost certainly was practiced during the Silla period (668-935). As for the oftenmentioned martial arts practices of the *hwarang*, a patriotic Silla period "fraternity" of youth, we have few specifics. They are said to have practiced Confucian virtues and the "six arts," which originally included archery and charioteering (they likely substituted horsemanship and possibly other martial arts, especially swordsmanship, for charioteering, a Chinese skill which had died out long before and which, in any case, was ill-suited to Korean terrain) (Il, 1995: 353-56; Yi, 1955: 15; Shin, 1963: 8).

Korean martial arts were probably strongly influenced by Chinese models from the Former Han on (206 BCE-24 CE). Although there are no descriptive Korean references to the martial arts prior to the *Koryo History* (completed in 1451, but covering the period 918-1392), its citations provide evidence that the Koreans had maintained a strict distinction between wrestling and boxing in the military, similar to the Chinese pattern, and that, slightly different from the Chinese, they also treated boxing as a formally recognized military sport or entertainment in a manner similar to wrestling. This practice was continued at least into the fifteenth century as confirmed in the *Veritable Records of the Yi Dynasty* (Yasiya, 1972; Yijo Sillok, 1953;

Gwahakwon, 1961). These records mention another military sport, also pronounced *subak* in Korean or *shoupai* in Chinese, which was probably akin to boxing. There are references to a similar skill, *paizhang*, during the Chinese Southern and Northern Dynasties period (420-589). In the *Elucidation of Names* (c. 25 CE.), *pai* is defined as *bo* (as in shoubo or subak) in hitting "above" (probably upper torso—chest and shoulders—and head) as in the Japanese sumo technique called *tsuppari*. In at least one instance, this skill was used to test soldiers for entry into the elite guards unit (*bangbakdae*) (Gwahakwon, 1961: 85, 210, 359; Li, 1936: 4a-4b; Liu, 1985: 2b).

Left: *Liangxian*—a bamboo infantry defensive support weapon supposedly designed by General Qi Jiguang for use in small unit tactics against Japanese pirates (probably never used by Koreans). Right: Staff and flail. All illustrations are taken from *Muye Dobo Tongji* (*Encyclopedia of Martial Arts Manuels*) combined with Chinese-Hangul labels. Courtesy of S. Henning.

Outside the military, as in China, boxing was practiced by the common folk on festive occasions. For example, annual competitive boxing bouts were held in the seventh month (according to the lunar calendar) in Unjin County, near the border of North Cholla and South Chungchong Provinces, while wrestling matches were held in a couple of locations in Seoul during the fifth month (No, 1958: 594; Yi, 1991: 99, 225).

As with the Chinese, archery was important to the Koreans and, similar to other groups on China's borders such as the Mongols and Manchus, the Koreans preferred the composite bow so convenient for equestrian use (the Chinese used the crossbow as well as the composite bow), and they practiced archery both on foot and from horseback. Similar to the Chinese, the Koreans also stressed use of the spear as the long weapon of choice on foot and from horseback. They bound spear tips with leather for competitive bouts. The *Veritable Records of the Yi Dynasty* also mention sword practice.

Sometimes training sessions resulted in fatalities when soldiers armed with wooden spears were pitted against elite guards armed with wooden swords

(Gwahakwon, 1961: 88, 99, 358, 362, 400, 405, 703). The record becomes murky during the sixteenth century, a period characterized internally by intense factional conflicts and neglect of military affairs, and externally by increased military use of firearms in China and especially in Japan, and which culminated in turbulence caused by Japanese invasions. Then, during the end of the eighteenth century, King Jongjo displayed a renewed interest in military affairs and commissioned a book on martial skills, which was completed by Yi Dok-Mu in 1790 under the title *Encyclopedia of Illustrated Martial Arts Manuals* (Yi: 1970).

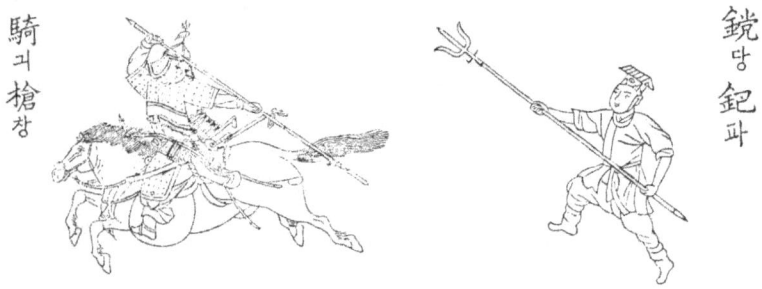

Left: Equestrian spear. Right: Trident.

Left: Boxing (*kwonbop*), copied from General Qi Jiguang's 32 boxing forms. Right: Equestrian crescent moon halberd.

Yi Dok-Mu's encyclopedia offers a fairly comprehensive view of traditional Korean and Chinese martial arts practices that were, in military terms, effectively outmoded at the time of publication. It mixes research from numerous Chinese sources, including Ming general Qi Jiguang's (1528-1587) *New Book of Effective Discipline* (c. 1561), together with contemporary Korean practices, and includes illustrated routines, on foot and from horseback, for broadsword (a cross between cutlass and saber), flail, and a variety of poled weapons such as spear, trident, crescent halberd, and others. The chapter on boxing (*quanfa* in Chinese, *kwonbop* in Korean, *kempo* in Japanese) is taken primarily from General Qi Jiguang's manual, but mixes in a couple of illustrations from a manual on escape and seizing techniques (the possible Chinese precursor to Japanese jujutsu) with Qi's original 32 boxing forms. It is possible that a combination of Chinese boxing and seizing techniques similar to those shown in Qi's manual influenced *taekyon*, a nineteenth century Korean sport described as employing "flying foot" and grappling techniques (Yi, 1970: ch. 4, 479-512; No, 1974: 145). The term *taekyon* or "push the shoulders" (not *taekkyon*, which appears to be based on lack of knowledge of the Chinese characters or an attempt to disassociate it from possible foreign origins) infers a technique possibly similar to that used in *tsuppari, paizhang,* and *shoupai*. While takyon is referred to as a distinctive fighting sport like subak, the term originally may have only been meant to describe a specific subak or *kwonbop* technique to put an opponent off balance. We are told that its association with undesirable activities such as revenge fights and gambling resulted in its prohibition and demise.

Left: Native country (Korean) sword.
Right: Long spear.

Both Koreans and Chinese had a healthy respect for the Japanese sword and Yi Dok-Mu's encyclopedia includes a section on Japanese sword techniques. Explaining that the terms for sword and knife had become intermixed, Yi presents as "native country sword" a routine using a weapon similar to the Chinese single-edged, curved broadsword (*dao* or knife in Chinese terminology) (Yi, 1970: ch. 2, 357-373).[1] Yi also associates traditional Korean sword practice with the story of Huang Chang-rang, who is said to have been a subject of the Silla kingdom. Huang supposedly learned sword dancing at the age of seven, entered the Paekche kingdom, where crowds gathered in the city to watch him perform. His fame brought him to the attention of the Paekche king, who had him perform at court. Huang assassinated the Paekche king in the midst of his performance, was executed in

Paekche and mourned as a hero in Silla and, from that time, the folk custom of performing a masked sword dance began (Yi, 1970: ch. 2, 357-373; No, 1958: ch. 21, 347).²

Although the references to traditional Korean martial arts are scattered and there are large gaps in information for some periods, one can see from the foregoing that it is still possible to piece together a broad outline which generally reflects Chinese influence. The Koreans appear to have modeled their military martial arts system on that prevailing as early as the Chinese Han period (206-220) and to have retained the term *subak*, originally associated with that period, through the fifteenth century, long after the Chinese terminology had changed. However, the term for wrestling changed from *kakjo* to *kakryuk* (Chinese, *jueli*; colloquial Korean, *sirrum*) during the Yi period (1392-1910) (Gwahakwon, 1961: 358; Yijo, 1953: juan 4, 50).

The historical evidence allows us to believe that traditional martial arts were part of Korean military training, and were practiced by individuals in the countryside, as late as the nineteenth century (for comparison, some traditional practices continued in the Chinese military until 1902). However, they appear to have been almost totally abandoned by the beginning of the twentieth century.

The evidence does not allow us to say, as some claim, that the traditional military skill, *subak*, was directly related to taekwondo or that "taekwondo is a martial art independently developed over twenty centuries ago in Korea."³ However, we can say that a couple of forms called subak were practiced there over the centuries and that takyon may have represented techniques associated with subak or kwonbop. Even modern takyon proponents refer to Chinese General Qi Jiguang's forms in the *Muye Dobo Tongji* in tracing their skills—this only tends to support the argument for Chinese influence (Yi, 1990). In any case, takyon does provide a slender thread tying in "traditional" skills with the emphasis on kicks in taekwondo. Taekwondo, for the most part, though, appears to be a post-Korean War product, developed primarily from what the Koreans called *tangsoodo* (karate) introduced during the period of Japanese rule.⁴

The traditional Korean martial arts are but a vague memory and taekwondo a symbol born in the cradle of modem Korean nationalism, a fact which should be kept in mind as we approach the 2000 Olympics in Sydney, in which taekwondo will be a featured sport.

Chinese, Korean, and Japanese References

Chonui Samguk Sagi	全譯三國史記
Dongguk Sesigi	東國歲時記
Gujin Tushu Jicheng	古今圖書集成
Hanguk Cheyuksa Yongu	韓國體育史研究
Hanshu Yiwenzhi Jiangshu	漢書藝文志講疏
Hwarangdo Yongu	花郎道研究
Jixiao Xinshu	紀效新書
Kokuri Hekiga Kofun to Kikajin	高句麗壁畫古墳と歸化人
Koryo Sa	高麗史
Muye Dobo Tongji	武藝圖譜通志
Nan Shi	南史
Samguk Yusa	三國遺事
Shinchong Tongguk Yoji Sungnam	新增東國輿地勝覽
Shiming	釋名
Wubei Zhi	武備志
Yijo Shillok	李朝實錄
Yijo Shillok Pullyujip	李朝實錄分類集

Chinese, Korean, and Japanese Terms

bangbakdae	防牌隊	Former Han	前漢
dao	刀	Huang Chang-Rang	黃倡郎
hwarang	花郎	hwarang	花郎
jujutsu	柔術	King Jongjo	正祖
kakjo/juedi	角觝 角抵	Koguryo	高句麗
kakryuk jueli/sirrum	角力	Koryo	高麗
karatedo	空手道 唐手道	North Cholla	全羅北道
kwon/quan	拳	Paekche	百濟
kwonbop/quanfa/kempo	拳法	Qi Jiguang	戚繼光
paizhang	拍張	Sokkuram	石窟庵
ryuksa/lishi	力士	South Chungchong	忠清南道
subak/shoubo	手搏	Southern & Northern Dynasties	南北朝
subak/shoupai	手拍	Tang	唐
sumo	相撲	Three Kingdoms	三國
taekyon	托肩	Unified Shilla	新羅
taekwondo	跆拳道	Unjin County	恩津縣
tangsoodo/karatedo	唐手道	Yi	李
tode/tangshou/tangsu/karate	唐手	Yi Dok-Mu	李德懋
tsuppari	突っ張り		

Notes

[1] According to Mao Yuanyi, the Koreans also faithfully maintained traditional Chinese double-edged straight sword skills which had gone into disuse in China. In his *Encyclopedia of Military Preparedness* (Wubei Zhi, 1621), Mao claims "...those who are interested can find it in Korea, where the forms and techniques are fully intact. Indeed, we know it is lost in China and must be sought among the... surrounding peoples..." However, Yi pointedly questions Mao's claim, noting that, in any case, there was no evidence of this over one hundred years later.

[2] "Sword dancing" is the traditional Chinese term for sword practice, which was especially popular during the Tang, roughly contemporary with the height of the Korean Silla period.

[3] www.rpi.edu/dpt/union/taekwan/public_html/history.httml, p. 1.

[4] Use of the term *tangsoodo* is surrounded by ambiguity. In Korean it means "way of Tang hands," referring to the Chinese Tang dynasty (618-960). In Japanese, the Chinese characters for tangsoodo are pronounced karatedo and also mean "way of Tang hands" (or "Chinese hands"), but since the Chinese characters for both "Tang" and "empty" are pronounced *kam* in Japanese, the term can also mean "way of the empty hand." This is now the preferred Japanese usage, although the former usage appears to have been more common when karate was first introduced to the Tokyo martial sports community from Okinawa in the 1920's (to confuse matters further, the Okinawans, who generally admit the Chinese origins of karate, originally used the *on* or so-called Chinese pronunciation of "Tang," so they pronounced karate as *tode* (long "a"). This usage distances the art from its Japanese connection and therefore would be more acceptable to Koreans, but the fact remains that taekwondo owes more to Japanese karate and less to traditional Korean martial arts than some Koreans care to admit.

References

Chen, Menglei. (1977). *Gujin tushu jicheng* (*Encyclopedia of ancient and modern literature*) Vol. 71. Taibei: Dingwen Shuju.

Gu Shi, (Ed.). (1987). *Hanshu yiwenzhi jiangshu* (*Annotated Han history bibliographies*). Shanghai: Guji Chubanshe.

Gwahakwon. (1961). *Yijo Sillok Pullyujip* (*Classified index of the veritable records of the Yi Dynasty*), Vol. 4 (Military Matters). Seoul: Gwahakwon.

Il, Yon. (1995). *Samguk yusa* (*Memorabilia of the Three Kingdoms*) (2d ed.). (Kim Pong-Du, Trans.). Seoul: Gyumunsa.

Kim, Un-yong. (1978). *Taekwondo*. Seoul: Korean Overseas Information Service.

Li, Yanshou. (1936). *Nanshi* (*Southern history*). Shanghai: Zhonghua Shuju.

Liu, Xi. (1985). Shiming (Elucidation of names). In *Sikuquanshu huiyao* (*Complete library of the four treasuries*) Vol. 78, juan 3. Taibei: Taiwan Shijie Shuju.

Ministry of Foreign Affairs Republic of Korea. (1956). *Korean arts, Vol. 1 painting and sculpture*. Seoul: Ministry of Foreign Affairs Republic of Korea.

Mizuno, Masakuni. (1972). *Kokuri heikiga kofun to kikajin* (*Koguryo ancient tomb wall murals and naturalized persons*). Tokyo: Yuzan Kaku.

No, Sa-sin. (1958). *Sinchong Dongguk yeji songnam* (*New expanded Dongguk gazetteer*). Seoul: Dongguk Munhaksa.

No, Sun-song. (1974). *Hanguk cheyuksa yongu* (*Korean physical culture history research*). Seoul: Munsonsa.

Shin, Sa-guk, (Ed.). (1963). *Chonui Samguk sagi* (*Complete translation of the History of the Three Kingdoms*). (Kim Chong-Kwon, Trans.). Seoul: Sonjin Munhwasa.

Yasrya, Munhaksa. (1972). *Koryo sa* (Koryo history). Seoul: Yasiya Munhaksa.

Yi, Dok-mu. (1970). *Muye dobo tongji* (Encyclopedia of illustrated martial arts manuals). Seoul: Hakmungak. Original dates from 1790.

Yi, Hyon-gun. (1955). *Hwarangdo yongu*. Seoul: Munhwasa.

Yi, Sok-ho. (1991). *Choson sesigi* (Korean annual customs). Seoul: Dong-munson.

Yi, Yong-bok. (1990). *Hanguk muye–Taekkyon* (*The Korean martial art–Taekyon*). Seoul: Hak Min Sa.

Yijo sillok (Veritable records of the Yi Dynasty). (1953). Tokyo: n.p.

chapter 2

The History and Development of Taekyon
by Robert W. Young

The famous "Dae Kwai Do" painting from the Seoul National University Museum collection. It was created by Hyesan Yusuk in 1846, shows ssirum wrestlers and taekyon practitioners performing for spectators. *Photos courtesy of R. Young*

Introduction

The origins and histories of the Korean martial arts have long been subjects of heated debate. Proponents of nearly every style claim theirs is the one historical art of the Korean people, but very few can prove their lineages reach more than fifty or sixty years back into the nation's history. Instead of offering tangible proof or logical argument to support their stories, modern Korean masters rely only upon oral histories passed from teacher to student. When one considers Korea's fierce nationalism and its general attitude that Korean culture is superior to all others, especially that of Japan, reliance upon word-of-mouth does not suffice in these matters.

Although Korea has valiantly struggled to retain its own identity while enduring the cultural onslaught of neighboring China and Japan, many more cross-cultural influences have occurred than most Koreans will ever admit. A great deal of Korea's culture, including much of its martial arts prowess, originated in China. Additional mainland influences came to the peninsula early in the thirteenth century when Mongolian armies invaded and occupied

Korea for more than 150 years (Han, 1970: 179). When the Mongols left, many of their customs and military technologies stayed behind. Among the lesser known Chinese and Mongolian influences are the Buddhist martial arts, Mongolian wrestling, and Mongolian archery (Lee Y. B., 1988, interview).

Contrary to what is generally believed in the West and vehemently argued in Korea, most so-called Korean martial arts are not original creations. A few owe their existence to skills imported from neighboring China during the past several hundred years, but most grew out of Japan's turn-of-the-century occupation (Lee Y. B., 1992, interview). Concerning Korean martial arts during the post-World War II developmental period, Y. H. Park writes, "For many years, a variety of Korean martial arts styles existed throughout the country. These styles varied from one another according to the influence each had absorbed from the numerous Chinese and Japanese styles . . ." (1989: 4). Seo In-sun writes that, after World War II, "Korean martial artists tried to revive Korean martial arts . . . but due to the heavy influence of the Japanese, many of these arts basically imitated Japanese movements and names" (1987: 44). These writers are the exception; most other Koreans refuse to admit any Japanese influence whatsoever.

A few martial arts scholars in Korea defy mainstream opinion and openly postulate that *subak* (*soo bahk*), the only fighting art mentioned in Korea's oldest records, was an ancient, comprehensive system with roots in northern China. Evidence supporting the contention that subak originated outside Korea is provided by Chinese records that list *sho buo* (Chinese pronunciation of subak) as an ancient martial art in the northern part of the country (Xu, 1989, interview). Probably within the past two thousand years, subak spread into Korea and found rapid acceptance first in the military and then in the populace. Once established in Korea, the system became divided into striking skills called *taekyon* and grappling skills called *yusul* (yoosool), and the two subsets eventually formed separate martial arts. Evidence suggests that yusul may have influenced the development of Japanese *jujutsu* (*yusul* and jujutsu are written with the same Chinese characters) but then died out on the Korean peninsula (Draeger and Smith, 1969: 76). Taekyon survives as the only fighting system descended from the ancient art of subak.

Martial Arts in Ancient Korea

During the millennium from about 500 BCE to about CE 500, great advances in human thought and civilization took place: Laozi and Confucius philosophized in China, the Buddha taught in India, and Jesus Christ preached in the Middle East. Not coincidentally, masters of most Korean martial arts claim their style's history dates from this period of great human creativity. As soon as one style puts forth such a historical statement, other arts are forced to do the same, for to say otherwise would be to admit that a competing style is more traditional, and, in the eyes of the public, more legitimate.

In his authoritative text titled *Subakdo Dae Gam*, Hwang Kee, founder of modem subakdo/tangsoodo, captioned a full-page photo of Baekdusan, a volcanic mountain on the border of North Korea and China, with the statement that Tan'gun, the ancestor of the Korean people, had taught young Koreans *kwonbak*, a forerunner of subak (1970: 14). Scholars generally believe, however, that Tan'gun never even existed. Historian Han Woo-keun calls Tan'gun "the mythical progenitor of the Korean people" (1970: 12). Author Robert Nilsen wrote that the legend of Tan'gun tells of the ancient ancestor's birth in 2333 BCE after a god changed a bear into a woman and impregnated her.

That Hwang, respected author and head of a worldwide martial arts organization, could make such a statement illustrates an important aspect of the Korean character and its penchant for making exaggerated historical statements. We can see how absurd claims are pushed further and further back into history, in this case more than 5,300 years, in an attempt to outdo the competition. All assertions regarding the history of martial arts require tangible evidence for corroboration or, at the very least, testimony from people who are not promoting their own martial arts. From this perspective we will examine Korean martial arts throughout the ages.

It should be noted that many Korean writers use the terms *subak* and *taekyon* somewhat interchangeably when describing martial arts prior to the Yi Dynasty. In reality, subak is the correct term for the martial art of this period because the name taekyon was not recorded until the eighteenth or nineteenth century. Over the centuries, subak has been called *subak-hi*, *subak-ki*, and *subyeokta*; taekyon has been known as *takkyeon*, *gak-hi*, *gak-sul*, and *bigak-sul* (Song, 1983: 19). Further illustrating the way some Koreans imprecisely apply one style name to other martial arts is Hwang Kee's use of the term subak-ki to describe the martial arts of historical Korea, Japan, Thailand, Burma, Indonesia, Malaysia, Laos, India, and China. The English translation of his book uses the term tang soo do because that appellation is more popular in the West. In this chapter, the term subak will be used until the period when historical records specifically name taekyon.

Koguryo Dynasty

Researchers generally believe subak was first practiced in Korea in the northern regions of the Koguryo Dynasty (37 BCE-CE 668). The territory, extending hundreds of miles north of the Yalu River, now forms part of Chinese Manchuria. Early in the twentieth century, Shin Chae-ho (1880-

1936), a Korean scholar exiled to China, wrote that Koguryo people practiced subak, swordsmanship, spear-fighting, and horseriding (Lee Y. B., 1990: 38).

In 1935 archaeologists discovered proof of ancient martial arts in several burial mounds near the town of Jian in China's Jilin province. It is now believed the tombs were erected by Koguryo dynasty Koreans between 3 and 427. The oldest physical evidence of martial arts in Korea is painted on the walls of three of these tombs: Gak Jeo Chong, Sam Shil Chong, and Mu Yong Chong (Oh, 1991: 7). Richard Chun writes that the murals indicate that people of the Koguryo Dynasty practiced subak as a martial art (1975: 10). Y. H. Park agrees: "Evidence of the practice of taekyon [subak] has been found in paintings on the ceiling of the Mu Yong Chong, a royal tomb from the Koguryo dynasty" (1989: 1). Choi Hong-hi, the father of modern taekwondo and a noted scholar of Korean martial arts, writes that the mural in Gak Jeo Tomb was painted during the reign of the tenth king of Koguryo and showed subak sparring (1972: 18).

Despite depictions in tomb art and occasional mentions in government records, scholars have been unable to determine exactly what techniques or fighting methods comprised subak. Records of the Koguryo Dynasty, most of which were not written until the Yi Dynasty (1392-1910), suffer from a lack of detail. Tomb paintings show generic poses and primitive techniques not easily identified as part of any modern martial art (Song, 1983: 17). The evidence indicates empty-hand fighting arts were practiced in Koguryo, but we cannot know for certain what they were or how closely they are related to modern styles.

This guardian deity carved in stone is located in China's Yun'gang Buddhist caves. For centuries, Korean culture was influenced by the Chinese. Their imprint can be easily seen in the aesthetic realm, in Buddhist sculpture as well as in martial art theory and practice.

Silla and United Silla Dynasties

The Silla Kingdom (57 BCE-CE 668), located in the southern portion of the Korean peninsula, received its first taste of northern subak from a battalion of soldiers and advisors sent by Koguryo. Park writes:

> After Silla appealed for help against the continual harassment by the Japanese pirates, King Gwanggaeto, the 19th in the line of Koguryo monarchs, sent a force of 50,000 soldiers into neighboring Silla to help the smaller kingdom drive out the pirates. It is at this time that taekyon [subak] is thought to have been introduced to Silla's warrior class.
>
> (1989: 2)

The citizens of Silla developed a great affinity for subak and refined the skills into a more effective military art. It was embraced by the military and widely taught throughout the kingdom. Park continues:

> These taekyon-trained warriors became known as the hwarang. They adopted taekyon [subak] as part of their basic training regimen. The hwarang . . . were encouraged to travel throughout the peninsula in order to learn about the regions and people. These traveling warriors were responsible for the spread of taekyon [subak] throughout Korea during the [United] Silla dynasty, which lasted from CE 668 to CE 935. (1989: 3)

This Korean Buddhist mural shows a
guardian deity holding a symbolic sword.

The *hwarang* (flowering knights) were a group of aristocratic teenage boys selected for their physical beauty and bodily strength. Han described their development as a "survival of the youth bands of tribal times . . . dedicated . . . to preparing to serve the state in war" (1970: 60). When the hwarang were not engaged in ritual song and dance, they drilled in the arts of war, primarily swordsmanship, archery, and spear-fighting. Secondary training included empty-hand striking and grappling techniques. The eventual unification of the three kingdoms—Silla, Paekche, and Koguryo—into the United Silla Kingdom attests to the warriors' combat efficiency.

No records specifically describe the martial arts of the hwarang fighters. They probably called their empty-hand striking and grappling skills subak, just as Koreans had for the previous several hundred years. It is uncertain if they had a special term to denote their weapons techniques. Lee Yong-bok asserts that it is ridiculous to believe that the hwarang relied mainly upon empty-hand martial arts in battle, as many Korean masters argue. Empty-hand skills would certainly have been but a minor adjunct to their military training and battlefield survival (Lee Y. B., 1988, interview). Therefore, we cannot say subak was the martial art of the hwarang; most likely it was merely one portion of their combat repertoire.

The hwarang's greatest contribution to the fighting arts was more spiritual than martial. Before the hwarang's existence, Korean fighting skills lacked a philosophical dimension. Their dedication to Mireuk Buddha (Sanskrit: Maitreya), the Buddha of the Future, caused this to change (Covell, 1982: 96). Han writes, "Quite often Buddhist monks were instructors of the hwarang. The monk Won Gwang, in fact, was the author of the famous *Sesok Ogye*, or *Five Tenets*" (1970: 61). Composed around 602, this work constituted the Way of the Hwarang:

> Serve one's king with loyalty.
> Look after one's parents with filial piety.
> Treat one's peers with trust.
> Withstand enemy attacks with courage.
> Terminate life with discrimination.

The *Five Tenets* spiritually strengthened the knights and, by augmenting their fighting skills with Buddhist philosophy and moral precepts, transformed them into true martial arts. Some argue that only then did subak and the various weapons systems cease to be merely methods for destroying enemies and become true martial arts with philosophical value and an attitude of charity and compassion. Choi Hong-hi agrees: "It appears that the warriors of hwarang added a new dimension to [subak] by . . . infusing the principles of the hwarang-do. The new mental concept. . . elevated foot fighting to an art" (1972: 18).

A recent version of the
Kumkang Yuksa image (In Wang)
stands beside the road leading
to Korea's Sukulam Grotto.

Another often-cited example of Korean martial arts during the Silla dynasty is the Kumkang Yuksa Buddhist images. In a chapter about Korean fighting arts, authors Draeger and Smith write, "The statues of Kumkang Kwon at the entrance to the [Sukulam] . . . show typical fighting postures" (1969: 74-75). Likewise, Choi Hong-hi writes, "The statue of Kumkang Yuksa, a famous warrior, [stands] in Sukulam, a stone cave built in the age of Silla. Notice the similarities in form between the Kumkang Yuksa and present day taekwondo" (1972: 17). Even Hwang Kee includes in the English version of his textbook under a photo of Kumkang Yuksa a caption reading "Statue of a General from the Shin Ra [Silla] Dynasty practicing subak-ki" (1970: 11).

In reality, the Kumkang Yuksa statues have no relationship to martial arts. Archaeologists have discovered these relatively common images across Buddhist Asia, from India to China to Korea. They actually portray Buddhist guardian deities, called *Vajradhara* in Sanskrit. Lee Yong-bok writes, "The In Wang statues [Kum-kang Yuksa] are from China and India; they are not evidence of Korean martial arts." Lee explains that both guardians originally held a spear in their hands, but when the images were transplanted to Korea, artists did not replicate the weapons. The resulting clenched hands resemble closed fists, thus appearing as empty-hand martial arts poses (1990: 47). Had the spears been reproduced, those who argue that the statues are in martial poses might not be so insistent. Even if die-hard proponents insist the carvings are actual martial poses, their documented presence in China and India would indicate that Silla-dynasty fighting arts had originated in one of those countries, not in Korea.

Koryo Dynasty

As the United Silla Dynasty gave way to the Koryo Dynasty (935-1392), subak continued to fare well among members of the Korean military. Numerous historical records in the *Koryo Sa* (*History of Koryo*) briefly mention subak while describing official court functions and military training (Song, 1983: 17, 29; Oh, 1991: 7). Another historical text reported that, during the twelfth century, a man named Eui Mu was skilled in subak and loved by the sixteenth king of Koryo. Because of his martial arts ability, Eui Mu was promoted to general (Hwang, 1970: 40).

According to Hwang, another book records that King Chung Hye (r. 1339-1344) watched a subak performance as part of a military celebration (1970: 40). The soldiers so impressed the king that he sought out the most skilled instructors and began to practice the art. Shortly thereafter, popular empty-hand fighting competitions pitted five-soldier teams against each other. These events, called *obyeong subak-hi*, helped make subak better known among government officials who had the opportunity to observed these spectacles (Lee, Y. B., 1990: 52).

Subak's popularity did not last long, however, for the next king, Chung Mok (r. 1344-1348), outlawed its practice by civilians. He was motivated by the high incidence of onlookers wagering outrageous prizes, including money, houses, even wives on subak matches. Chung Mok set the penalty for betting on subak matches at one hundred strikes across the buttocks with a wooden paddle. Recipients of the beatings often died of infection (Lee, Y. B., 1990: 52).

Koryo Dynasty soldiers practiced subak as a compulsory supplement to weapons training. For this reason, it is not surprising that the focus of the art shifted towards quick and lethal attack methods. The military organized national competitions to motivate troops to develop their combat skills and fitness levels and to evaluate them for promotion (Choi, H. H., 1972: 19).

Researchers have discovered no specific records of any other martial arts in the early Koryo Dynasty, so we can assume that subak still included all its original kicks, punches, joint-locks, throws, and pressure-point strikes. Even though evidence indicates the art spawned the grappling sport of ssirum as early as the Koguryo Dynasty, subak training in the Koryo Dynasty still consisted of striking and grappling (Kim J. R., 1990: 20).

Yet during the later Koryo Dynasty, or possibly during the early years of the Yi Dynasty, masters specializing in various aspects of subak went their separate ways. Park writes, "Subak as an art became fragmented and diffused throughout the country, and its practice continued to decline until only incomplete remnants remained" (1989: 3). Sources indicate that *yusul*, a soft art ultimately derived from the same Chinese art of *shobuo* (subak), became popular in the twelfth century, then became extinct early in the nineteenth century (Draeger and Smith, 1969:76). In 1945, historian An Ja-san wrote a text titled *Chosun Mu Sa Yeong Ung Jeon* in which he details the lives and exploits of military heroes of the Chosun (Yi) Dynasty. According to Choi Hong-hi, An's book states, "The yu sul school was known under the name of subak-ki . . ." (1972: 19).

Sometime after yusul separated from the subak repertoire, the subset of remaining subak skills, which contained mostly striking techniques, became known as taekyon. At times, pronunciation of the same two Chinese characters varied to *takyon*, but both meant "push shoulder" (Chung, 1990, interview). In the English version of his text, Hwang succinctly describes the origin of the kicking art: "Taekyon developed from ancient tang soo do [subak]" (1970: 13). Contrary to some historical accounts of the development of the Korean martial arts, subak/taekyon was never called tangsoo, kongsoo, or taekwon. Those arts actually developed independently and quite recently and were based mostly upon the Japanese interpretation of Okinawan karate (Lee Y. B., 1989, interview).

Yi Dynasty

Scholars cannot pinpoint the exact date on which the Yi Dynasty (1392-1910) text titled *Man Mul Bo* (a.k.a. *Je Mul Bo*) was written, nor can they verify that Yi Seong-ji, the suspected author, was actually responsible for those four volumes of Chosun Dynasty lore (Oh, 1991: 7). However, they have examined in detail the work's contents (history, law, medical learning, etc.) and found a short entry under taekyon. It may have been the first time the fighting art's name was rendered in Hangul, the phonetic script created in 1446 by King Sejong. Before that, the name had always been written in Chinese as subak (Lee Y. B., 1990: 68-69).

As the Yi Dynasty progressed, specific references to taekyon began to occur more frequently. Historical documents tell how the third king of the dynasty (r. 1401-1408) recruited experts in taekyon, ssirum wrestling, and archery to help organize the army (Choi H. H., 1972: 19). The thirty-second volume of *Tae Jong Shil Lok* records that, beginning in 1410, the court organized several military parades which featured taekyon demonstrations. Centuries later, such a performance may have inspired Kim Hong-do, a popular eighteenth-century Korean folk artist, to create his royal palace grounds painting of a crowd of aristocrats observing a taekyon sparring match (Taekwondo, 1989: 29).

A better-known Korean folk painting dating from the later Yi Dynasty again shows taekyon and even refers to it by name. Its title is *Dae Kwai Do*, or competition painting, and it now hangs in the Seoul National University

Museum. Painter Hyesan Yusuk, who lived from 1827 to 1873, is thought to have created the work around 1846 (Oh, 1991: 34, 52). Dae Kwai Do depicts two men sparring and two others grappling, while a group of *yangban*, or aristocrats, looks on. The painting's legend specifically names the arts as *taekyon* (spelled takkyon) and ssirum wrestling.

The *Chosun Wang Jo Shil Lok*, a historical book detailing the lives of Yi Dynasty kings, often mentions taekyon (Oh, 1991:7). It describes how, in the middle and later parts of the dynasty, soldiers' examinations included spear fighting, archery, and taekyon, and how front-line soldiers were sometimes selected from among winners of taekyon fighting competitions (Lee Y. B., 1990: 59-62).

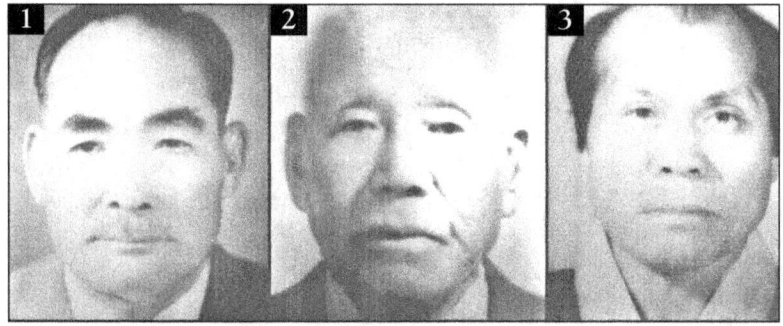

1) Taekyon Master Kim Hong-shik, born July 6, 1895, once headed the Gurigae taekyon school. 2) Song Duk-ki renowned master of taekyon and *kung sul* (traditional archery), was named Human Cultural Asset. 3) Shin Han-seung was also honored as a Human Cultural Asset because of taekyon.

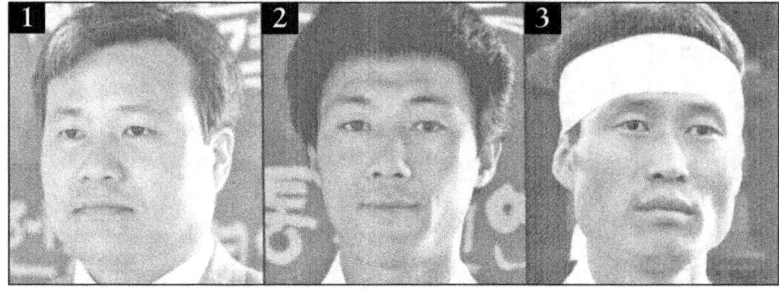

4) Lee Yong-bok founded the Pusan-based Korea Traditional Taekyon Research Association in 1985 and the Seoul-based Korea Taekyon Society in 1990. 5) Son Il-hwan now heads the Korea Traditional Taekyon Research Association in Pusan. 6) Chung Kyeong-hwa heads the Korea Traditional Taekyeon Society and teaches in Chunju.

One of the world's oldest martial arts instructional manuals was reportedly authored around 1759 by a Korean named Cheok Gye-gwang. Titled *Muye Dobo Tongji*, it describes and illustrates in exact detail every fighting skill Cheok could research. Although one chapter focuses on empty-hand fighting, most of the book discusses weapons techniques, including broadsword, sabre, spear, halberd, trident, and others too obscure to name (Kim G. S., 1990: 10-11).

Nearly all modern Korean arts claim *Muye Dobo Tongji* as proof of the historicity of their styles. Yet many researchers point out that most of the weapons discussed are distinctly Chinese and that even the empty-hand techniques resemble the Chinese way of fighting. In his book, Song Duk-ki called Cheok Gye-gwang a Chinese national and discredited citation of Cheok's work as proof of Korean martial arts (1983: 18). Song's assertion gains support from a Chinese book which says, "Qi Jiguang [Chinese pronunciation of Cheok Gyegwang], a well-known general, compiled a book dealing with sixteen different styles of bare-hand exercises and another forty of spear- and cudgel-play, each with detailed explanations and illustrations" (Chinese Martial Arts, 1987: 4). Both the Korean and the Chinese works feature nearly identical drawings and were written using Chinese characters, but neither mentions subak or taekyon. Instead, empty-hand skills are called *kweon beop*, pronounced *chuanfa* in Chinese (Xu, 1989, interview). For these reasons, *Muye Dobo Tongji*, whether an original Korean work or an early example of plagiarism, cannot be reliably cited as historical evidence for subak/taekyon or any other style.

Decline of Taekyon

The introduction of firearms initially suppressed martial arts practice as guns replaced swords, bows, and spears both in military training camps and on the battlefield. Officers could see little need for their men to practice seemingly antiquated empty-hand fighting skills when more advanced weaponry was becoming available. But later, when guns could not be produced in sufficient quantities and never became available to the masses, taekyon enjoyed a slight resurgence in popularity (Lee Y. B., 1988, interview).

Much more devastating was the pressure exerted against martial arts when Neo-Confucianism, a resurgence of the social guidelines and values taught by the Chinese sage Confucius, grew during the latter half of the Yi Dynasty (1392-1910). Just as taekyon was beginning to find increasing popularity among the general population, Neo-Confucianism brought about a drastic decline of all martial arts practice outside the military. As the phrase "favoring the arts and despising arms" came into vogue, scholasticism and civil service received official support, while physical and combative activities were disdained (Lee Y. B., 1980: 191).

In an account in *Chosun Sang Go Sa*, Shin Chae-ho confirms that taekyon, once famed throughout the Koryo Dynasty, nearly died out during the Yi Dynasty (Lee, Y. B., 1990: 71; Song, 1982: 17). In *Chosun Mu Sa Yeong Ung Jeon*, An Ja-san also intimates that taekyon was waning (Oh, 1991: 7). In spite of these pressures, the art did not succumb. Park writes that taekyon, facing Neo-Confucianism's effect on the government and military, was able to survive only because of its popularity among the general public (1989: 3). A large number of practitioners spread across the peninsula insured the art's survival, if only in remote locations. In his writings about the later Yi Dynasty, Shin noted that archery and taekyon contests were still held in some locations to test the skill and strength of soldiers (Choi, H. H., 1972: 18).

Hwang Kee speculates that another reason for the art's near downfall may have been that taekyon acquired a less-than-honorable reputation (1970: 41). He says that, after returning from Manchuria in 1939, he heard from elderly Koreans stories in which young people learned taekyon for criminal purposes and often formed street gangs. He writes that taekyon was looked down upon because it did not teach discipline and that it only contained non-specific offensive-defensive techniques called *gongbang beop*. It is difficult to determine exactly how much of Hwang's account is fact and how much is merely an attempt to promote his own subakdo/tangsoodo style by discrediting taekyon in the public eye. Although taekyon's criminal connection remains a possibility, no other researcher has mentioned it.

Taekyon After 1910

Imperial Japan established a foothold in Korea during the end of the nineteenth century, then formally occupied the nation from 1910 to 1945. To comply with orders to suppress all aspects of Korea's cultural identity, they restructured Korea's educational system to parallel their own, gave Japanese names to Korean citizens, and decreed that Koreans speak only Japanese. All native Korean fighting arts, which the Japanese felt were likely to foment rebellious, anti-Japanese feelings, were naturally prohibited. Those who disobeyed the new laws were often rounded up and executed.

During this time, taekyon's existence was tenuous. Koreans desperately wanted to preserve this important aspect of their heritage, but by doing so they risked death. In 1925 King Kojong, the last Yi Dynasty monarch, decided to help save what he judged a valuable piece of history. He confidentially ordered Hong Mong-hwa to formulate a taekyon instructional book. Four taekyon practitioners traveled to the city of Chungju to demonstrate their techniques, and Hong began writing and illustrating. Unfortunately, Korean scholars do not know what happened to the manual; they know of its creation only because Hong's son witnessed the process and later recounted it to Lee Yong-bok (Lee, Y. B., 1990: 77).

Although Japanese troops greatly contributed to the waning of an already weakened art, their occupation of Korea did inspire a few people to persevere in their practice. Several taekyon practitioners scattered around the country continued to train, but the men most responsible for the art's continuance in the twentieth century lived in Seoul (Lee, Y. B., 1990: 60). Because of the Japanese patrols, the men always trained at night or in remote locations. Lee Yong-bok says little evidence exists to support claims that taekyon was used in organized guerrilla warfare against Japanese forces (1988, interview). However, at least one account has been confirmed: Kim Gu, resistance leader and head of the Korean Independence Party, writes in his autobiography that he was a taekyon expert and that he often fought the Japanese in hand-to-hand combat matches (Lee, Y. B., 1990: 75).

Three main taekyon schools existed during this time: the Gurigae dojang under Pak Mu-gyeong, who began practicing taekyon in 1880; the Chongno dojang under Im Ho, who also began in 1880; and the Wangshimni dojang under Pak Tul-baek, a student since 1845. Each master taught essentially the same taekyon skills. Students were few because of the Japanese prohibition. In 1900 Kim Hong-shik began learning taekyon from Pak Mu-gyeong and later succeeded him as head of the school. Likewise, Shin Jae-young, who had begun to learn the art in 1880, replaced Pak Tul-baek in the Wangshimni dojang. Under Im Ho, at least eleven students trained; the senior was Song Duk-ki (Oh, 1991: 22). [See Lineage Chart, p. 37]

This photo shows Shin Han-seung
in the 1970's demonstrating
a *don dae*, or taekyon form.

Song was born in Seoul on January 19, 1893, and began studying taekyon when he was twelve (Song, 1983: 8, 21). Evidently, Song never had time to absorb all the skills of his instructor during their six years together, for, in a later conversation with student Lee Yong-bok, he admitted he did not learn all that Im Ho knew and regretted that part of taekyon died with Im. Song never enjoyed the position he later inherited as the savior of taekyon; he wished only to practice without interruption from Japanese police (Lee, Y. B., 1988, interview). Yet soon he would become one of the two most important taekyon masters of modern times. Korea was liberated from colonial rule at the close of World War II, and Koreans were finally free to teach whatever martial arts they wanted. Interest in taekyon and other arts did not immediately increase because people were preoccupied with their newly found freedom and with the rigors of trying to rebuild their country. Because so many tasks demanded attention, taekyon practice would have been a luxury for most people. Song Duk-ki was one of the few who found time to train (Song, 1983: 9).

Political tensions rose during the late 1940's and early 1950's until war finally broke out in 1953. Once again, the nation fell into chaos, disrupting whatever plans taekyon masters had for the art's revival. Song said that, during the tumultuous 1950's, he was only able to meet and practice taekyon with Kim Hong-shik on several occasions (Oh, 1991: B). No records tell of the lives of the other taekyon students and masters during the Korean War.

The first recent taekyon demonstration in public occurred during a national police martial arts competition on March 26, 1958, the birthday of former President Rhee Syngman. Rhee greatly enjoyed the special demonstration organized by Im Ho and Kim Seong-hwan but felt sorry that taekyon was dying out in its homeland (Song, 1983: 21). A presidential bodyguard who knew Song Duk-ki personally later told him how the president desperately wanted the art to continue for future generations. Song began looking for a more qualified taekyon master to fulfill Rhee's request, but he could find none. As far as Song knew, only he, Kim, and the elderly Im Ho continued to practice taekyon.

In 1971, a newspaper article about Song appeared in the *Hanguk Ilbo* (Oh, 1991: 21). The article introduced taekyon and Song to a public that was mostly unaware of the traditional style and caught the attention of Shin Han-seung, who had been practicing taekyon sporadically since he was fourteen. He immediately departed for Seoul to meet Song (Oh, 1991: 164). The two developed a cordial relationship, and for the next six months Shin traveled back and forth from Chungiu to Seoul to learn additional taekyon skills he had not acquired from his former instructors, Kim Hong-shik and Shin Jae-young.

Born on May 9, 1928, Shin had trained in amateur wrestling and judo in his youth. Therefore, he was well acquainted with the teaching methodologies of combative arts. In 1971, he decided to systematize into an easily taught curriculum all the taekyon skills he had learned from his three teachers. Later the same year, he and Song applied to the Korean Cultural Property Preservation Bureau to become *In qan Mun Hwa Jae*, or Human Cultural Assets.

Shin Han-seung practiced
taekyon kicks even in his 60's.

June 1, 1983, brought victory to Shin and Song as the government of the Republic of Korea named them Human Cultural Assets because of their unique taekyon skills and efforts to preserve the art. The titles were automatically rescinded when both men died in 1987 (Oh, 1991: 35). Taekyon's claim to be Korea's first martial art was also acknowledged when the government officially recognized it as Intangible Cultural Asset #76. No other Korean martial art, before or after, has attained this status.

Since taekyon became an Intangible Cultural Asset, two groups in Korea have vied for control of the style: the Pusan-based Korea Traditional Taekyon Research Association, founded by Lee Yong-bok in 1985 and the Korea Traditional Taekyon National Headquarters under Chung Kyeong-hwa in Chungju. Both organizations are endeavoring to make the art more widely known in Korea and eventually around the world.

Until now, however, efforts to propagate taekyon have met with limited success. The phenomenal growth of taekwondo, aggressively promoted by the Korean government and military, has eclipsed the lesser-known taekyon. Additionally, taekyon authorities have regularly refused to organize tournaments on the grounds that, though it might help popularize the style, it could relegate taekyon to the status of merely another Korean martial sport.

In 1991, the Pusan-based taekyon organization succumbed to the pressure and organized its first team-sparring tournament. However, they managed to create a system of rules quite different from those used by other Korean martial arts. The event met with enough success and media coverage to persuade the organizers to hold taekyon tournaments annually, in hope of gaining more exposure.

To affirm in the public eye taekyon's differences from the many Japanese-influenced Korean martial arts, modem taekyon authorities refuse to adopt the Japanese-style *gi* (Korean: *dobok*) worn by students of other Korean styles, including taekwondo, tangsoodo, hapkido, kuksul, yudo, and yusul. Instead, taekyon students and teachers wear white *hanbok*, the traditional Korean work clothes, and *jipshin*, sandals made of woven rice straw.

Modern taekyon practitioners also avoid the Japanese system of colored rank belts. Taekyon does use rankings, but only those who attain the level of first *dong*, the traditional Korean equivalent of the Japanese *dun*, wear a belt. Students under the rank of first degree belong to *jjae* levels instead of the more common *geup* (*kup*) rankings of taekwondo. Once a student attains the first degree ranking, he dons a blue sash, knotted on the side and worn under the uniform blouse.

Arguments Against Other "Ancient" Korean Martial Arts

When one is searching in Korea for modern descendants of ancient subak, the only system for which historical evidence exists, it is necessary to examine those other styles claiming to have inherited subak's skills and techniques or to have been associated with the hwarang warriors. Only when those arts have been eliminated from consideration can one logically maintain that taekyon is the only existing martial art descended from the ancient form of combat. Those contemporary martial arts to be examined include subakdo/tangsoodo, taekwondo, kuksul, hwarangdo, and yusul.

Subakdo

In Seoul, Korea around 1945, Hwang Kee founded modern subakdo, better known in the West as tangsoodo. He claims to have based the style on Chinese kuksul, which he says he had learned in Manchuria starting in 1936. Hwang's use of the term *kuksul* [or *kuk sool*] (national skills), a generic Chinese term for martial arts, in no way refers to the style currently taught by the Korea Kuk Sool Association or the Korean Kuk Sool-Hapkido Association, for Hwang's stay in Manchuria occurred long before Seo In-sun and Suh In-hyuk formed Kuk Sool Won in 1961 (Seo, 1987: 4).

Among the reasons Hwang gives for traveling to Manchuria, one of the most important was to practice martial arts without interference from Japanese troops. Yet he seldom mentions that the Japanese Imperial Army had moved into Manchuria in the 1890's, defeated the Russians in the Russo-Japanese War of 1904-5, and immediately seized the Russian territory. They took the rest of Manchuria in 1931, renamed it Manchukuo, and established a puppet regime under figurehead Emperor Puyi (Schirokauer, 1989: 449, 502, 526-528). It is doubtful the Japanese forces in Manchuria would have been any less oppressive than their counterparts in Korea, who strove to stamp out every aspect of indigenous culture and national identity. Only with great difficulty can one imagine Hwang learning traditional Korean martial arts or even Chinese kuksul while under the watchful Japanese eye.

Magazine writer Sohn Tae-soo interviewed Hwang Kee in 1991 and uncovered a number of previously unknown facts about the creation of modern subakdo. He writes that Hwang's "serious training in martial arts started when he began to work for a Japanese railway company in Manchuria after graduating from high school" (1991, October 5, 26-27). Hwang was evidently unable to learn much about traditional Korean arts before he departed his homeland, and once in Manchuria, he closely associated with the Japanese on the job.

Sohn reports that Hwang was reassigned to Korea in 1939 and then established the Moo Duk Kwan school in Seoul. He writes that Hwang

> named the martial art tang soo do (way of the China hand) for a practical purpose. Written in Chinese characters, the Korean name of tang soo do could be read the same as Japan's karate. With traditional Korean martial arts all but dead under the colonial suppression of Japan, he says he had no choice but to make his martial art sound similar to a Japanese one and thus make it familiar to the public. Then he changed the name to subak-do in 1955 (1991: 27).

Although he references different years, Park gives a similar account that begins after an unsuccessful attempt in 1953 by Hwang's Korea Tang Soo Do Association to join the Korea Athletic Association. He writes, "In June 1960, Korean Soo Bahk Do Association, named after the traditional Korean martial art, was formed by Hwang to replace the Korean Tang Soo Do Association" (1989: 13).

Thus it seems that Hwang Kee originally chose to name his martial art tangsoodo, either because the name was written the same as karatedo, the art he probably studied in Manchuria, or because he wanted to evoke mental images of a Japanese style in Korea. Later, perhaps then to avoid being associated with the Japanese and to facilitate recognition by the government, Hwang resurrected the historical Korean name of subak, but added the "do" suffix so common among Japanese style names (e.g. karatedo, kendo, judo, budo, kyudo). Researcher Seo In-sun writes that use of the "do" suffix for martial art names originated in Japan and that Korean historical texts list no fighting art names ending with "do." Instead, Koreans used "ki," "sul," or "yea" suffixes, and records always refer to Korean martial arts as *mu sul* or *mu yea* (Seo, 1987: 43).

Furthermore, the resemblance between Hwang Kee's subakdo/tangsoodo and Okinawan karate continues to draw attention. Chris Thomas examined several modern Korean arts and concludes tangsoodo "bears the greatest conformity to Shotokan" (1988, November: 30). Although the evidence indicates that Hwang learned Okinawan karate from the Japanese in Manchuria and then adopted the name subakdo as an afterthought, he refuses to reinforce his claims of learning Chinese/Korean rooted martial arts by naming his instructors or explaining how they influenced the development of subakdo/tangsoodo. Sohn writes:

> Instead, he says it is not an appropriate time to talk about such issues. 'What I can tell you at the moment is I had no one to teach me subak-do. I revived subak by doing research alone while touring around the nation." A breakthrough in his research came when he came across a book on martial arts in Seoul National University's library in 1948. (1991: 26-27)

Here, Hwang clearly admits to having had no subak instructor. He claims to have learned the style from a book written by an eighteenth century Korean scholar who wished to describe a fighting art supposedly founded five thousand years ago (Sohn, 1991: 27). Yet Hwang will not produce the book to back up his story. These facts, coupled with the aforementioned observations about Hwang's life and his martial art, leave little reason to accept his claim that subakdo/tangsoodo is a direct descendent of ancient subak.

Taekwondo

Most taekwondo masters maintain their style originated in Korea more than two thousand years ago, and to prove it nearly every taekwondo text includes photos of the aforementioned Koguryo Dynasty tomb paintings, the Kumkang Yuksa statues, and even the Dae Kwai Do painting. Koreans are adamant that the roots of taekwondo, their national martial art, are purely Korean. Any attempt to argue otherwise is met with disbelief, disapproval, or outright anger.

Very few Koreans will admit how great an influence the Japanese had on taekwondo's development. Choi Hong-hi, widely regarded as the father of the art, created in 1972 a comprehensive text titled *Taekwon-do: The Korean Art of Self-Defence*. In it, he writes of taekwondo, "This style is primarily based on taekyon, subak, and karate . . ." (p. 20). Corcoran and Farkas researched the art and concludes, "Modern taekwondo is a combination of the *hyung* (patterns) of its ancestral combative arts, taekyon and subak, and the kata (formal exercises) of the Okinawan Shuri and the Naha schools of karate" (1983: 130). Taekyon experts deny that taekwondo has incorporated any taekyon techniques but are reluctant to publicly say so in Korea because of the negative repercussions of mud-slinging (Chung, 1990, interview). However, Corcoran's assertion that taekwondo includes Japanese techniques currently enjoys more support among researchers and comparative martial artists.

Choi Hong-hi never revealed just how much of his style was derived from karate. Regarding his own martial arts training, Choi says he was sent to Japan in 1937 to further his education. In Kyoto, he ". . . met a fellow Korean, Mr. Kim, who was engaged in teaching the Japanese martial art, karate." After practicing for two years, Choi earned the rank of first-degree black belt. About these karate skills, Choi writes, "These techniques, together with taekyon (foot techniques), were the forerunner of modern taekwondo" (1972: 513). Choi claims to have learned taekyon from a famous calligraphy master named Han Il-dong prior to creating taekwondo (1972: 19, 513). Yet taekyon researchers Lee Yong-bok and Chung Kyeong-hwa both confess that their efforts to locate dojang records of Han have failed (Lee, Y. B., 1990, interview; Chung, 1990, interview).

Kim Soo, a taekwondo grandmaster who resides in the U.S.A. and teaches at Rice University and the University of Houston, is one of the few outspoken Korean researchers willing to elaborate on the history of his art. In an interview conducted by *Tae Kwon Do Times* magazine, he said:

> I do know, however, that it is fair to say that the modern era of Korean martial arts, 1945 to present, has been most heavily influenced by Okinawa and Japan. This is because the Japanese prohibition of martial arts during their occupation of Korea all but extinguished the styles which had been practiced in Korea. After the liberation of Korea at the end of World War II, the martial arts instructors who began teaching in Korea were primarily Korean nationals; some who had learned Shotokan karate, and some who had learned Shudokan during their stay in Japan. It is these styles which are the genesis of modern taekwondo. (1992, May: 50)

Some researchers contend that the similarity of the terms taekwondo and taekyon proves a causal relationship. Yet it is only when transliterated into English that the name taekwondo appears similar to taekyon. In Korean or Chinese characters, there is no relationship whatsoever. Taekwondo comprises "tae," or kick, "kwon," fist or punch, and "do," the way. The term taekyon is actually composed of "taek," meaning push, and "gyeon," meaning shoulder. Perhaps Hwang Kee best sums up taekwondo's history and development: "Taekyon is not related to the current taekwondo" (1970: 41).

Thus, we see that many aspects of taekwondo's history attest to the influence of the Japanese and their martial arts. The art's name is but a convenient term adopted by consensus on April 11, 1955, after General Choi Hong-hi proposed it (1972: 515). Its incorporation of the "do" suffix mirrors the Japanese practice of naming arts. After an exhaustive comparison of the *hyung* (kata) of taekwondo and Shotokan karate, Chris Thomas wrote that taekwondo, heavily influenced by the Japanese prior to World War II, was originally "little more than transplanted Shotokan" (1988, November: 30). Little reason remains for considering taekwondo a remnant of ancient subak.

Kuksool Won

A third style, that taught by the Korea Kuksool Association, is often claimed to be closely related to Korea's ancient fighting arts. Proponents say their art dates from far back in Korean history, but like practitioners of other styles, they have failed to produce tangible evidence. Although Kuksool Won Chiefmaster Seo In-sun writes that kuksul comes from a mixture of ancient tribal martial arts, royal court martial arts, and Buddhist martial arts, Kim Il-nam, Chairman of the Korea Hapkido Association in Seoul, dismisses the story. Instead, he argues that kuksul is a mixture of the self-defense skills of hapkido and the weapons techniques of *shippalgi*, a Korean interpretation of Chinese gongfu (Kim I. N., 1990, interview).

Although most kuksul authorities insist their style has ancient, purely Korean origins, they deny any historical relationship between kuksul and taekyon/subak or taekwondo. Barry Harmon, Secretary General of the World Kuksool Association in California, writes, "Taekyon is one of the foundation arts of taekwondo, not of kuksul" (1990, personal correspondence). Therefore, the possible existence of a relationship between ancient subak and modern kuksul warrants no further discussion.

Hwarangdo

California resident Lee Joo-bang teaches a martial art Westerners know as hwarangdo, but of which most Koreans have never heard. The comprehensive system includes hand and foot strikes, trapping, grappling, pressure-point usage, weapons techniques, and healing methods. The style purports a history plagued with inconsistencies, one which cannot link it to ancient subak or even the hwarang warriors.

Supreme Grandmaster Lee Joo-bang, fifty-eighth heir to the title and head of the U.S.-based organization, presides over an art that appears virtually indistinguishable from hapkido and kuksul. Some minor differences can be found, but the major components of the style—some 3,600 joint-locks, throws, and escapes—are identical. Several Korean martial arts authorities, including Kim Il-nam, state that Lee was a hapkido expert in Korea prior to moving to the U.S. (1990, interview).

Lee's historical claims begin with Won Gwang's development of "a system of martial arts that was in harmony with his concept of the laws of nature" (Lee J. B., 1980: 4). He writes that the Buddhist monk taught the martial art to boys who later formed the hwarang. Yet all other historical accounts of the contribution of Won Gwang stop at his formulation of the aforementioned *Sesok Ogye*, the *Five Tenets*; no mention is made of the monk's creation or teaching of a martial art.

Lee provides little additional developmental details besides a few noble Silla Dynasty warrior tales taken from the *Hwarang Segi*, the *Records of the Hwarang* (Lee J. B., 1980: 6-9). None of the passages in the *Hwarang Segi* or the *Samguk Yusa*, another ancient Korean text containing stories of the hwarang, mentions the name of any fighting style (other than archery) or discusses any specific techniques.

Lee's version of his art's history next jumps to the Yi Dynasty as he explains how Japanese pressure forced practitioners of hwarangdo into isolated Buddhist temples. It was in one of those monasteries, Lee maintains, that he met the fifty-seventh grandmaster of hwarangdo, a monk named Suahm Dosa, and began training. Lee writes:

> In 1969 Grandmaster Suahm Dosa died and the position of grandmaster was passed to Joo Bang Lee. This position made Joo Bang Lee the inheritor of the ancient martial art and the Supreme Grandmaster in an unbroken line of succession lasting over 1,800 years.

Lee first claims that his art was created by the monk Won Gwang (whom the *Samguk Yusa* lists as having lived in the late sixth century [Ha, 1986: 279]). Lee then says he is the successor to an unbroken lineage that began in the second century, leaving some four hundred years of history unexplained. He cites no records mentioning hwarangdo as a martial art, and texts by masters of other styles fail to list hwarangdo as a historical name of any Korean art. Draeger and Smith write, "Hwarang itself was not a combat technique or fighting art" (1969: 72). Because historians of the style cannot argue a link to subak or the hwarang, hwarangdo cannot at this time be considered a direct relative of any ancient Korean martial art.

Yusul

Modern yusul, as taught by the Korea Yoo Sool Association in Pusan, has so far presented little evidence to support its claim that founder Kim Mu-jin learned the ancient Korean grappling art in Japan because it had become extinct in Korea (Kim, M. J., 1988, interview).

Kim's organization has also kept the name *yawara*, which he says is mearely an alternative name for yusul. Yet in Japan, the Chinese characters for *yusul* can be pronounced as *yawara*, though they most often are pronounced as jujutsu. Although the presence of technical similarities between the joint locks and pressure-point strikes of yusul and jujutsu has not yet been researched, a cursory comparison points to a great similarity. It seems that, once again, a modern derivative of hapikido, or perhaps even a totally Japanese art, has adopted the historical name of an ancient Korean fighting art for publicity and commercial success.

These arguments disqualify as possible descendants of original subak all modern Korean martial arts except taekyon. Hwang Kee himself admitted that taekyon developed from ancient subak while making no such clims about other modern styles (1970: 13). Since neither his own art nor taekwondo can be reliably linked to ancient subak and since they closely resemble Japanese karate, they must be disqualified as having Korean roots. Kuksul, which may be an offshoot of hapkido, makes no claims to have descended from subak, and proponents of hwarangdo, another possible offshoot of hapkido (or of kuksul), have little historical basis for their claims that this was the art of Silla's hwarang warriors. Modern yusul, whose founder admits to having trained in Japan, cannot now be linked to ancient yusul, the grappling subset of original subak. Only taekyon remains as a surviving remanent of the ancient fighting art of subak. It is quite certain that the taekyon system was not completely transmitted, as Song Duk-ki himself admitted, but it is all we have.

Taekyon Theory and Technique

To conclude this examination of the art of taekyon, it is necessary to discuss ways in which its practice differs from that of other Korean fighting styles. If no significant differences existed, it would be pointless to argue the originality and uniqueness of the style solely upon the basis of name. If, however, major dissimilarities are noted, it will provide further support for taekyon's historical claims.

Left: Taekyon's ground fighting techniques include disarming a knife-wielding attacker. Right: Son Il-hwan demonstrates an outside front kick (*jjae chagi*), one of taekyon's most popular techniques.

Unlike many hard, external Korean arts which are best suited for younger students, taekyon can be practiced well into old age. Because all movements are intended to harmonize with the structure of the human body, techniques are natural and minimally stressful. Part of the reason for this stems from the art's abandonment of normal warm-up and stretching exercises. Instead, the basic techniques, interspersed with brief series of hand pats along the length of tight muscles, provide the necessary muscle stretch and circulation boost. Song Duk-ki proved taekyon's therapeutic side effects by training daily until the age of ninety-four. Shin Han-seung continued until he died at the age of sixty.

Like other martial arts, taekyon teaches the use of *ki*, or internal energy, to augment physical power. One method for releasing ki is through a *kihap*, the forceful exhalation of air at the moment a technique is performed. However, taekyon's kihap differs from that of all other Korean and Japanese arts. Instead of a short, loud explosion of noise, taekyon students make a soft but forceful "eekeh" sound which, they claim, comes from the traditional Korean fighting arts. The short, guttural shout used by taekwondo practitioners and other Korean martial artists originated in the Japanese arts, they argue (Lee Y. B., 1988, interview).

A basic principle of taekyon sparring is to attack hard with soft, and soft with hard. To illustrate, a punch to an opponent's jaw, while undoubtedly effective, will inflict considerable pain on the puncher. It is, therefore, more sensible to strike a hard target with a softer weapon, the heel of the hand, for example. Conversely, taekyon teaches that an attack to the fleshy mid-section is more effective if the striker uses a hard weapon such as the knee or elbow. Lee Yong-bok explains that, unlike most other fighting styles which advocate performing a linear technique and then completing it at the point of impact, taekyon teaches students to continue techniques past their potential point of impact. During a taekyon offensive move, a limb does not strike and return; instead, it travels in a natural arc and returns without having to stop and retrace its path (Lee, Y. B., 1988, interview).

In a violent encounter, taekyon strategy teaches a person to stand directly in front of his attacker and move with a rhythmic motion that allows a quick, evasive slip to either side. In contrast to the linear movements in taekwondo and other Korean arts, the taekyon student's body constantly moves forward and backward, to the left and to the right. Lee Yong-bok describes this strategy as the first skill of taekyon: staying away from the attacker's weapons (1988, interview). According to this logic, evasion is superior to blocking because, as long as an opponent's attack fails to make contact, his power does not matter.

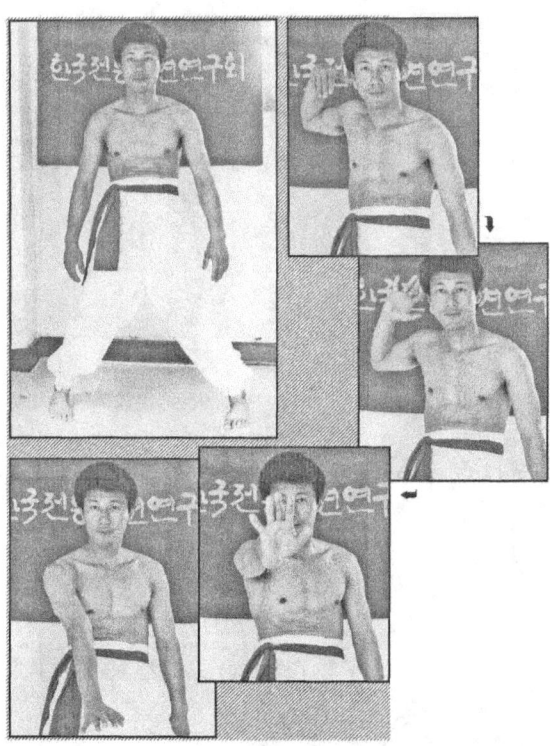

Son Il-hwan demonstrates taekyon's
abdominal breathing and ki-development exercises.

1) Taekyon also teaches close-range fighting as Pak Man-yup demonstrates with a *bak chigi*, or head butt. 2) Taekyon includes no conventional punching; instead the hands are use for, among other things, the *hangjeong chigi*.

3) Another open-hand strike to the throat is the *teok baegi*. 4) Chung Kyeong-hwa executes a *duru chigi*, part of a continuous series of downward chopping kicks to the chest.

5) Taekyon sparring often includes leg sweeps and take-downs such as the *ogeum chagi mit jungbang geori*. 6) In the *anjjang dari geolmyeo deot geori*, a take-down follows a sweep to the back of the opponent's supporting leg.

7a-b) Chung Kyeong-hwa performs a *hwalgae bal hoi mok japgi*, in which Chung traps Pak Man-yup's front kick, then delivers a *kal jebi* hand strike to his throat.

Taekyon fighters move with a rhythm which beginning students sometimes learn while traditional Korean drums and bamboo flutes keep time. This rhythmical motion into and out of attack range further differentiates the style from all others (Oh, 1991:15). Similar movements have been found in the *tal chum*, the centuries-old Korean mask dance (Lee Y. B., 1988, interview). Herein lies another of taekyon's differences from other Korean martial arts: during this continuous body motion, the arms constantly move up and down, out and back, and from side to side, confusing the opponent as to exact target locations. When combined with nimble footwork in four directions and occasional evasive jumping, a taekyon stylist becomes more difficult to hit.

Taekyon's kicks have proved so effective that the style does not even include among its hand strikes a traditional jab or reverse punch. These kicks are so legendary that, for hundreds of years, the name of the art was synonymous with foot-fighting. However, the kicks bear little resemblance to the typical spinning and jumping maneuvers glorified in tournaments and film. Instead, taekyon leg techniques are simple and direct, focusing upon linear moves but including limited usage of circular and spinning kicks. Lee Yong-bok says, "Taekyon has traditionally emphasized stepping and stamping techniques directed at the opponent's lower legs and feet" (1992, interview).

In contrast to the intensity of taekyon when it existed only for combat, modern practice limits the damage that may be inflicted upon fellow students. Lee explains the traditional rules of friendly taekyon competition, probably developed within the past one hundred years, as follows:

- Custom (greeting and bowing) comes first.
- Kicking above the neck is allowed.
- Pressure-point attacks are not allowed.
- Trapping with the hands is allowed.
- Light to medium contact is allowed.
- Jumping and kicking with both legs is allowed.
- Leg-grabbing and take-downs are allowed.
- Knocking out one leg with a kick is allowed.

(Lee Yong-bok, personal interview)

Under the system Shin Han-seung systematized, taekyon training progresses through three steps. The first is *honja ikhigi*, or training by oneself in basic movements and techniques. The second is called *maju megigi*, or practice of more difficult and realistic techniques with a partner. The third is *gyeon jugi*, or sparring. This last stage teaches what can only be learned in simulated combat when the defender does not know his opponent's actions or reactions beforehand (Oh, 1991: 16).

In conclusion, it seems obvious that taekyon is the only plausible candidate for the descendant of ancient subak. Its verifiable history of at least one hundred fifty years, during which its name was used in historical records, is far more thoroughly documented than that of any other Korean martial art. It is the only Korean fighting system that cannot be easily connected to modern Japanese and Chinese martial arts, and its skills and techniques greatly differ from those of other modern Korean styles. The evidence presented above persuaded the Korean Cultural Property Preservation Bureau that taekyon is a unique and historical martial art. Unfortunately, it is doubtful the arguments will ever convince masters or students of competing Korean styles that taekyon is Korea's oldest fighting art.

Taekyon Lineage in the 20th Century

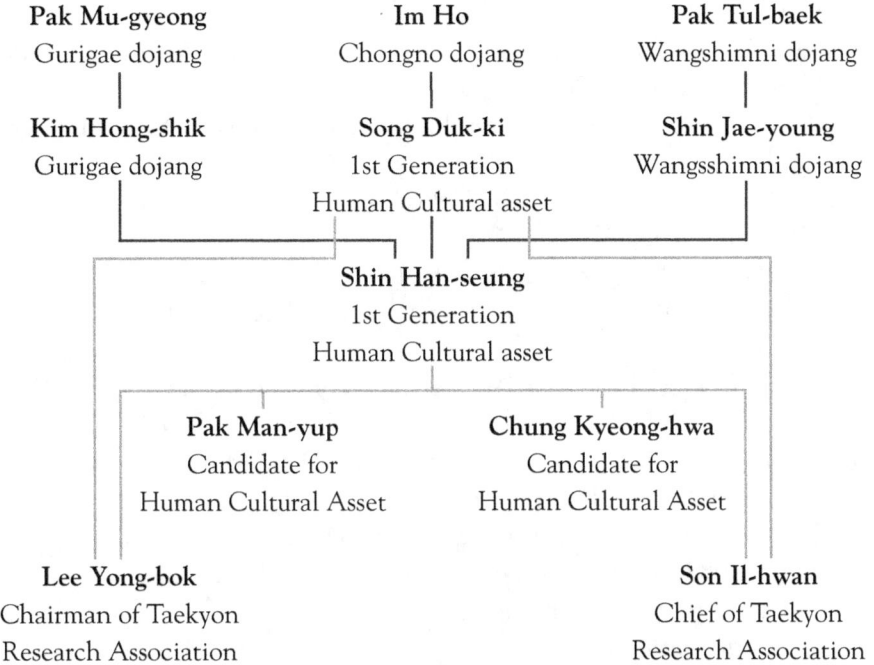

Note

Of the many Korean-English transliteration systems, two are widely used: the McCunes Reischauer system and the Ministry of Education system. Most Korean words in this chapter were written using the Ministry of Education system. For certain words, including the names of people, cities and well-known martial arts, the most widely recognized spelling has been kept. According to *Chosun Eo Dae Sa Jeon*, the *Great Dictionary of Chosun*, taekyon can be written in Korean as deok gyeon, taek gyeon, tae ggyeon, and tak gyeon (Oh, 1991: 13; (Song, 1983: 23). In English, taekyon has been rendered as taekkyun, t'aekkyon, taekgyeon, and taek kyon. In this chapter, it has been spelled taekyon for the sake of simplicity. The first syllable of the name is pronounced exactly like the English word "take." The second syllable is pronounced "gyun"; it rhymes with "fun."

References

Chinese martial arts. (1987). Beijing: Morning Glory Press.
Choi, H. H. (1972). *Taekwon-do: The Korean art of self-defence*. Ontario: International Taekwon-do Federation.
Choi, J. H. (1990, July). Personal interview.
Chun, R. (1975). *Moo duk kwan tae kwon do: Korean art of self-defense*.

Burbank, CA: Ohara Publications.
Chung, K. H. (1990, July). Personal interview. (1992, June). Personal interview.
Corcoran, J., and Farkas, E. (1983). *Martial arts: Traditions, history, people*. New York: Gallery Books.
Covell, J. C. (1982). *Korea's cultural roots*. Elizabeth, N.J.: Hollym International corp.
Draeger, D. F., and Smith, R. W. (1969). *Comprehensive Asian fighting arts*. New York: Kodansha.
Ha, T. H. (1986). *Samguk yusa*. Seoul, Korea: Yonsei University Press.
Han, W. K. (1970). *The history of Korea*. Seoul, Korea: Eul Yoo Publishing Company.
Harmon, B. (1990, November 19). Personal correspondence.
Hwang, K. (1970). *Su bak do dae gam*. Seoul, Korea: Han U Ri.
Kim, G. S. (1990). *Mu yea do bo tong ji*. Seoul: Dong Mun.
Kim, I. N. (1990, July). Personal interview.
Kim, J. R. (1990). *Ssirum gyo bon*. Seoul: Seo Rim Mun Hwa Sa.
Kim, M. J. (1988, July). Personal interview.
Lee, J. B. (1980). *The ancient martial art of hwarangdo, vol. 3*. Burbank, CA: Ohara Publications.
Lee, Y. B. (1988, October). Personal interview.
Lee, Y. B. (1990). *Hun guk mu yea taekyon*. Pusan, Korea: Shi Ro.
Lee, Y. B. (1990, August). Personal interview.
Lee, Y. B. (1992, May). Personal interview.
Meeting of minds: The grandmasters speak, part two. (1992, May). *Tae Kwon Do Times*, pp. 50-57.
Nilsen, R. (1988). *South Korea handbook*. Chico, CA: Moon Publications.
Oh, J. H. (1991). *Taekyon jeon su gyo bon*. Seoul: Young Eon Mun Hwa Sa.
Park, Y. H. (1989). *Taekwondo: The ultimate reference guide to the world's most popular martial art*. New York: Facts on File.
Schirokauer, C. (1989). *A brief history of Chinese and Japanese civilizations*. New York: Harcourt Brace Jovanovich.
Seo, I. S. (1987). *Kuk sool*. Pusan, Korea: Il Teo.
Sohn, T. S. (1991, October 5). Hwang Kee faithful to tradition in reviving soo bahk do since '45. *Newsreview*, pp. 26-27.
Song, D. K., and Pak, J. G. (1983). *Jeon tong mu sul taekyon*. Seoul: Seo Rim Mun Hwa Sa.
Taekwondo. (1988). Seoul: World Taekwondo Federation.
Thomas, C. (1988, November). Did karate's Funakoshi found taekwondo? *Black Belt*, pp. 26-30.
Xu, H. (1989, November). Personal interview.

chapter 3

Notes on the Historical Development of Korean Martial Sports: An Addendum to Young's History and Development of Taekyon

by Willy Pieter, Ph.D.

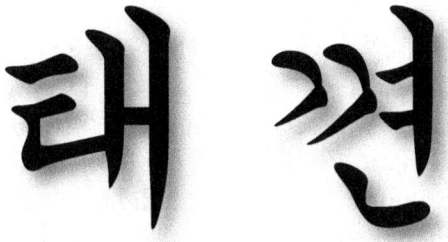

Introduction

Taekwondo* is presently one of the fastest growing martial sports in the world. Although scientific research is ongoing at the moment to study various characteristics of elite taekwondo athletes, such as endurance, leg strength, competition anxiety, and so on (Pieter, 1991; Pieter and Taaffe, 1992), little is known about the historical development of the sport. Popular instructional texts (e.g., Choi, 1972; Chun, 1982) would trace the origin of taekwondo and other Korean martial sports back to the Three Kingdoms: Koguryo (37 BCE-CE 660), Paekche (18 BCE-CE 660), and Silla (57 BCE-CE 935). More critical and objective studies, such as Young's (1993) recent article on the history of taekyon (taekkyon), have cast doubt on the accuracy of these claims. Even the much older *Muye Dobo Tongji* (Yi and Pak, 1970), which was reportedly written in 1790 (Kim, 1990; Lee, 1981), will not lend support to any historical claims concerning the Korean origin of modern martial sports found in Korea. On the contrary, the book is written in classic Chinese with a translation in classic Korean. The sections on unarmed *quanfa* (*kwonpop* in Korean and *kempo* in Japanese) are primarily descriptions of ancient Buddhist and Daoist health exercises. As indicated by Young (1993), there is no mention whatsoever of any of the names commonly associated with Korean martial sports. Korean sources seem to agree that caution is warranted when discussing the hwarang relative to any ancient Korean martial arts or modern Korean martial sports (Kim, 1990; Yi, 1979). The purpose of this chapter, then, is to add to Young's study and expand on some of his observations.

The Hwarang

Taekwondo and other Korean martial sports are very often thought to be derived from the hwarang group from the Silla dynasty (Choi, 1972); Chun, 1982; Corcoran and Farkas, 1983). This notion, however, is most likely erroneous as was pointed out elsewhere (Pieter, 1985; Young, 1993). The available historical sources seem to indicate that there is no reason to assume that the hwarang were in any way related to the development of taekwondo or any other Korean martial sport as the Japanese samurai were to the development of classical bujutsu and classical budo (Draeger, 1973; 1975). Actual usage of the word "hwarang" shows a wide variety of interpretations other than one solely of martial significance.

The word "hwarang" has been used for a brand of cigarettes, a bar in a hotel, the name of a musician, a youth corps and so on, and has become a symbol of modern Korea. Whatever the use, the "institution of the hwarang is [always] presented in an idealized and noble light" (Rutt, 1961: 2). The conception of the hwarang as a military cult did not become prominent until after World War II when the Japanese started to promote their idea of bushido (Rutt, 1961).

The best translation for *hwarang* is "flower boy" (Mathews, 1972; Rutt, 1961) and not "flower of youth" (Chun, 1982) or "flower of manhood" (Corcoran and Farkas, 1983) or any other similar rendering. This translation "is literal and does no violence to either Chinese or Korean grammar (the translation 'flower of youth' is certainly grammatically, and possibly semantically, false)" (Rutt, 1961: 7).

Most of the information on the hwarang can be gleaned from two main Korean historical sources: the *History of the Three Kingdoms* (*Samguk Sagi*) and the *Memories of the Three Kingdoms* (*Sambuk Yasu*) (Rutt, 1961). The *Sagi* was compiled by the soldier-statesman Kim Pu-sik (1075-1152) by order of King Injong of Koryo in 1145 while the *Yusa* was written a century later by the monk Iryon (1206-1289). The *Sagi* consists of twenty-eight books recounting in order the annals of Silla, Koguryo and Paekche, followed by three books of chronological tables, nine books of monographs, and finally, ten books of biographies. The *Yusa* also begins with a chronology, followed by stories of individuals and places. The *Yusa* is written in a style that is much less strict than the *Sagi* and contains more anecdotes, but it should not be disregarded as an historical account of ancient Korea (Rutt, 1961).

No further information on the hwarang is available from other historical sources, including Chinese dynastic histories. It should be realized that the prejudices of the writers of the *Sagi* and the *Yusa* "are very markedly demonstrated, and can save us from accepting a view of the nature of the hwarang that might otherwise be very one-sided" (Rutt, 1961: 15). Both sources, however, agree on the religious character of the hwarang. The hwarang became closely related to the Maitreya (the Buddha of the Future) cult (Henthorn, 1974). It is even mentioned that the Maitreya appeared as a hwarang (An, 1977).

The story of the hwarang, according to *Samguk Sagi*, is as follows (Rutt, 1961). The forerunners of the hwarang were the so-called *wonhwa*, or "original flowers," instituted by King Chinhung (r. 540-576) of Silla. Two pretty women by the names of Nammo and Chunjong were chosen to dance. These two women had some three to four hundred followers, who were taught filial and fraternal piety as well as loyalty and sincerity. The two women grew jealous of each other's beauty and Chunjong finally killed Nammo for which she, in turn, was put to death, while the followers of the women were dispersed. The king subsequently chose handsome boys from good and moral families, who were called "flower boys" (*hwarang*). They wore make-up and beautiful clothes, and just like the *wonhwa*, they also gathered a large group of followers. They sang, danced, made music and spent time in the hills and by the rivers (Rutt, 1961).

The primary goal of the institutionalization of the hwarang, which was basically a youth organization, according to Yi (1979), was to discover talent to be recommended to the royal court for entertainment. The author also observed that, although it is generally agreed that the hwarang originated somewhere around the first half of the reign of King Chinhung, it is also suggested that the hwarang may have existed during the reign of King Pophung (514-540) in 525.

According to the *Samguk Yusa*, King Chinhung chose pretty girls as wonhwa. They were taught filial and fraternal piety in addition to loyalty and sincerity. They apparently were very helpful in governing the country (no specifics are given regarding the exact manner in which they were "very helpful"). In the end, Nammo and Chunjong (the first Chinese character of Chunjong's name differs from the one in the *Sagi*), who had some three to four hundred followers, were chosen (as leaders?). Eventually, Chunjong grew jealous of Nammo and when the latter had taken too much wine, Chunjong took her to a river and killed her. Since Nammo's followers did not know where she had gone, they dispersed and mourned. However, someone knew what had happened and taught children to sing a song about the murder.

Chunjong was subsequently put to death and the king disbanded the wonhwa. After a few years, the king chose boys from good families, who were of good morals and named them hwarang (Rutt, 1961).

From the stories in the *Sagi* and *Yusa* it can be concluded that the hwarang were based on an earlier organization of women. These women were probably shamans or had shamanistic functions (Rutt, 1961). The hwarang had their monk-followers, who were their school teachers and who also took care of their moral education in addition to writing the lyrics of their songs (Yi, 1979). Evidently, the religious character of the hwarang has been accepted as a constant of this youth group.

It is not clear what the role of the martial arts was in the education of the hwarang. Yi (1979) observed the importance of making music, playing games and mountaineering in the training of the hwarang groups, the leaders of which were called *hwaju* and the followers, *nangdo*. However, Rutt (1961) related that the terminology used to identify the members of such groups is not precisely defined in the *Sagi* and the *Yusa*. Nevertheless, since the hwarang produced generals and soldiers and since they played a part in the unification of Korea, it can be assumed that they must have had some military training (among other things, probably archery and charioteering).

The hwarang were mainly recruited from the second highest level of Korean society at that time, the so-called *chin gol* (true bone) (Korean society was divided into so-called *bone-ranks* or castes determined by ancestry). The position of general and the highest civil posts were monopolized by the true bone (Henthorn, 1974). Concerning the relationship between the hwarang and their martial status, Rutt (1961) has observed that the hwarang "were a band of adolescents of high purpose, who could not avoid being both religious and at least quasi military, sometimes very military, because that was the nature and need of the society in which they lived" (p. 46). Lee (1975) has also mentioned that the hwarang supplemented the aristocratic army of Silla of which the king was commander-in-chief. "In emergency situations, members of the hwarangdo (followers of the hwarang) were drafted into the national army and sent off to war, . . ." (p. 10). In other words, the hwarang were not an independent army in themselves.

According to Rutt (1961), the hwarang became entertainers after the unification of Korea. They often specialized in one of the activities that they were engaged in, such as singing, dancing, poetry, and so on, when not participating in the wars that the old kingdoms of Korea had to endure. A name change seems to have taken place after the Silla period, however, and the hwarang were then called *sollang* and *kukson*. This change in name may be related to the location of the subsequent Koryo dynasty (918-1392), which was in the central and northwestern parts of the country, while the word "hwarang" survived longer in the southern and eastern parts where the original hwarang lived during the Silla dynasty (Rutt, 1961).

Etymology

In attempting to clarify the relationship between certain martial art practices and the hwarang, it may be helpful to trace the origin of some specific Korean martial terms that often link the two together. The etymology of some of the more popular Korean martial art terms associated with taekwondo have been presented elsewhere (Pieter, 1981). None of these terms would suggest any relationship with taekwondo as it is presently practiced in either Korea or anywhere else.

The best translation of the word "hwarang" has already been mentioned above. The following discussion is entirely based on Rutt's (1961) examination of the term. The original version of the word seems to have been *hwa* and was used as a title suffixed to one's name, while it was later replaced by the second half of the word *hwarang* (*rang* or *nang*). Variations of the word are *hwarangi* or *kwangdae*, meaning "well-dressed singer or dancer." The emphasis in these cases is on nice clothes and dancing. Other variations include *hwaryangnyon* (slut or prostitute) and *hwanyangnom* (playboy; lazy good-for-nothing). *Hwarang, hwarangi* or *hwaraengi* may also be used to indicate shaman or shaman's husband. Until the word hwarang was specifically used in relation to Korean martial arts and sports in the twentieth century, it had rather negative connotations.

Tangsoodo is the Korean pronunciation of the Chinese characters for Chinese (*tang*) hand (*su*) method (*do*), or "Tang hand way," which in Japanese is karatedo. As is well known, this was the original designation and meaning of *karatedo*, i.e., "China hand way" (Chinese way of the hands). In Japanese, the first character (i.e. *kara*) was used to denote something that was foreign, especially something from China. The Japanese adopted its use from the Chinese to signify the Chinese Tang dynasty (618-907). Later, when karatedo was written with a different first character, *kara* indicated "empty," which in Korean is *kong*. Karatedo in its present meaning of "empty hand way" is called *kongsudo* in Korean (Pieter, 1981).

Another name that is frequently related to taekwondo is *taekyon*, which is commonly translated as (an art of) "kicking" (Chun, 1976) or foot technique (Choi, 1972). Culin (1895) presents an insightful discussion of what taekyon probably entailed. According to the author, taekyon is a game that was also known in Japan, but probably not in Guangzhou (Canton). It is mainly a game with the legs in which the participants try to kick each other's feet from under him, although it is also possible to catch the legs with the hands and to throw the opponent. Taekyon in Korean is written in two syllables: *tae* and *kyon* (Kim, 1990; Lee, 1981). More than a decade ago, no Chinese characters could be found to write this word with (Pieter, 1981).

In the absence of Chinese characters, it is difficult to say anything definitive about the term. According to *The New World Korean-English Dictionary* (1979), *taekyon* means "kicking and tripping art (as a sport)." *The New World Dictionary* does not provide any Chinese characters for taekyon, but it does offer a synonym for the activity, i.e., *gakhui*, which in Chinese is written with two characters, the first character means "foot" or "leg" while the second means "to play." In other words, *gakhui* (spelled *gakhi* in Young's [1993] article) is a game played with the legs and the feet. This description would lend support to Culin's (1895) observations on taekyon.

It seems reasonable to assume that the naming of taekwondo was based entirely on phonetics, for although Korean words may be written with the same Korean characters and have the same pronunciation, they may have a totally different meaning depending on the original Chinese characters with which they were derived. For example, the Korean word *do*, may be written in Chinese with the character meaning "way," "method" or with another character meaning "nothing," "nil." Therefore, although *tae* in taekyon sounds the same as *tae* in taekwondo and is written with the same Korean characters, its meaning may be totally different. Only *gak* in gakhui comes close to *tae* in taekwondo as far as its meaning is concerned, but both words are written with different Chinese and Korean characters as well as pronounced differently.

Subak has been translated as "punching and butting" (Chun, 1976: 5). The first character, of course, means "hand." The second character means "to strike with the fist," "to box," "to punch" (Mathews, 1972; Nelson, 1972). As for "butting," this part of Chun's (1976) translation may not be accurate. Butting may be related to *bak ch'igi*, "striking with the head," but in this case, *bak* may have nothing to do with *bak* as used *subak* (Pieter, 1981).

Lee (1981) gave three more different sets of Chinese characters for subak. The first one of these seems to represent the same meaning as the characters used in the preceding paragraph, i.e., "to strike with the hand." The other two sets of characters, however, apparently have been chosen for purely phonetic reasons, for their meanings (see Mathews, 1972) do not relate to anything that has been discussed in the preceeding paragraph.

Of course, an etymological analysis like the one attempted here can only be used to indicate historical links and roots. It does not imply any particular martial activity actually done under a specific name. Cases in point were illustrated by Young (1993) in his discussion of hwarangdo and Hwang Kee's subakdo/tangsoodo. *Hwarangdo*, as the Way of the hwarang, may be compared to the later Japanese bushido as far as being a social/philosophical framework within which the hwarang would act (Yi, 1979). However, in its original usage, it did not necessarily include the martial arts as a way of life followed by the hwarang in the sense that the martial arts were followed by the Japanese warriors (*bushi*) and should certainly not be mistaken as referring to martial arts that were ostensibly practiced by the Silla hwarang. Further, although the Way of the hwarang was undoubtedly inspired by the *Sesok Ogye*, or *Five Secular Commandments*, this does not necessarily mean that the *Ogye* were typical of the hwarang institution. Though no documentary evidence is available to connect the *Sesok Ogye* to the hwarang, it may safely be assumed that the *Ogye* were typical of the age in which the hwarang lived and that they undoubtedly reflected the spirit of their times (Rutt, 1961; Yi, 1979).

The *Sesok Ogye* are a combination of Confucian and Buddhist teachings and were formulated at the end of the sixth century by Won Gwang (Yi, 1979), who became known a generation after King Chinhung, the founder of the hwarang (Rutt, 1961). According to the *Samguk Sagi* and *Samguk Yusa*, two young warriors (who later were killed in a battle against the army of Paekche [Yi, 1979]) approached Won Gwang and asked him for aphoristic guidelines to help them order their lives. Even though the two youths, Kwisan and Ch'wihang, were warriors, there is no evidence that they were hwarang (Rutt, 1961). It may be concluded that "however reasonable it may be to assume that the *Ogye* reflect the spirit of the hwarang, it is impossible, because of the dating, to regard them as a formulation of the hwarang code. It is more than likely that there was a great deal more to being a hwarang, especially from the religious and musical points of view, than is described in the *Ogye*" (Rutt, 1961: 64).

Bibliography

An, K. H. (1977). Silla Buddhism and the spirit of the protection of the fatherland, *Korea Journal*, 17: 27-29.

Choi, H. H. (1972). *Taekwondo: The Korean art of self-defense*. Toronto: International Taekwondo Federation.

Chun, R. (1982). *Advancing in taekwondo*. New York: Harper and Row Publishers.

Chun, R. (1976). *Taekwondo: The Korean martial art*. New York: Harper and Row Publishers.

Corcoran, J., and Farkas, E. (1983). *Martial arts: Traditions, history, people*. New York: Gallery Books.

Culin, S. (1895). *Korean games: With notes on the corresponding games of China and Japan*. Philadelphia: University of Philadelphia Press.

Draeger, D. F. (1975). *Classical budo*. New York: Weatherhill.

Draeger, D. F. (1975). *Classical bujutsu*. New York: Weatherhill.

Henthorn, W. (1974). *A history of Korea*. New York: The Free Press.

Kim, Y. O. (1990). *T'aekwondo ch'olhak ui kusong wolli*. Seoul: T'ongnamu.

Lee, C. W. (1981). *T'aekwondo kyobon*. P'umse P'yon, Seoul: Taehan

T'aekwondo Hyophoe.

Lee, K. B. (1975). Korea: The military tradition. In H. H. W. Kang (Ed.), *The traditional culture and society of Korea: Thought and institutions* (pp. 1-42). University of Hawaii, Honolulu: The Center for Korean Studies.

Mathews, R. H. (1972). *Mathews' Chinese-English dictionary.* (rev. American ed.). Cambridge, Massachusetts: Harvard University Press.

Pieter, W. (1981). Etymological notes on the terminology of some Korean martial arts. *Asian Journal of Physical Education, 4,* 1: 47-52.

Pieter, W. (1985). Korean hwarang and Japanese samurai: A comparison. In N. Miiller and J. K. Riihl (Eds.), *Sport history Olympic scientific congress 1984 official report* (pp. 75-80). Niedernhausen: Schors-Verlag.

Pieter, W. (1990). Performance characteristics of elite taekwondo athletes, *Korean Journal of Sport Science,* 3: 94-1 17.

Pieter, W. and Taaffe, D. (1992). The Oregon taekwondo research project: Results and recommendations. *Journal of Asian Martial Arts, 1* (1): 72-85.

Rutt, R. (1961). The flower boys of Silla (hwarang): Notes on the sources. *Transactions of the Korea Branch of the Royal Asiatic Society,* 1-66.

The new world comprehensive Korean-English dictionary, (1979). Seoul: The Si-Sa-Yong-o-Sa Publishers.

Yi, K. D. (1979). Silla hwarangdo ui sahoe hak chok ko ch'al. *Yoksa Hakpo,* 82: 1-38.

Yi, T. and Pak, C. (eds.). (1970). *Muye tobo t'ongji.* (rev. ed.). Seoul: Shinhan Sorim.

Young, R. W. (1993). The history and development of taekyon. *Journal of Asian Martial Arts, 2* (2): 45-69.

chapter 4

The Elevation of Taekyon from Folk Game to Martial Art
by Yung Ouyang, B.A.

*All photographs courtesy of the Dahmul Culture Center.
Photography by Ko You-sun.*

Introduction

The martial arts of East Asia (China, Korea, Japan) are known to be identified with certain elements, such as strong philosophical underpinnings and lineage systems, that establish their legitimacy. However, we must be careful not to allow our preconceived notions of what an East Asian martial art is supposed to be to prejudice or color how we view all martial art forms from those countries. Although in modern day Korea taekyon is looked upon with pride by many Koreans as being the indigenous martial art, it has not always been so. In fact, for much of its history, taekyon was considered a game played by commoners and was looked down upon as lacking in values. Taekyon traditionally was an art that did not exhibit many of the same elements as its counterparts in China and Japan, but only in its modern form has it become like other East Asian martial arts.

The Game of Taekyon

An often overlooked aspect of taekyon is that traditionally it was a game as well as a martial art. Although this aspect of the art has been mentioned before, understanding its significance in a fuller way will remove much of the confusion around it and richly enhance our understanding of taekyon. Although in the West it has been classified as a martial art, in reality taekyon is much more complex, and our understanding of it is obscured just because there is so little written material on it, and those persons from early in the century who are knowledgeable enough to be able to preserve it are few in number. Our understanding of it is also obscured by our preconceptions of what an East Asian martial art is supposed to be like. Taekyon cannot neatly be classified into the traditional Western categories of martial art, game, or dance; in its traditional form, it displays qualities of all three. In many ways, taekyon also displays qualities which do not fit in with our traditional definitions of martial art, game, and dance. This will be discussed in greater detail further along in the article, but now let's examine the evidence.

Terminology

Among the different names for taekyon and its parent art subak are such terms as *subak-hi*, *gak-hi*, *gak-sul*, and *bigak-sul* (Lee, 1990). The "*sul*" suffix of the terms *gak-sul* ("leg art") and *bigak-sul* ("flying leg art") denote the fact that taekkyon was an art or a skill. However, the "*hi*" suffix of the terms *subak-hi* ("game of subak") and *gak-hi* ("leg game") show that taekyon was also thought of as a game.

In his book *Games of Korea* (1895), anthropologist Stewart Culin includes a description of the object and rules of the game in a section entitled "Taik-kyen-ha-ki":

> Taik-kyen-ha-ki is a combat between two players, chiefly with the feet. They take their positions with their feet apart, facing each other, and endeavor to kick the other's foot from under him. A player may take one step backward with either foot to a third place. His feet, therefore, always stand in one of three positions. One leads with a kick at one of his opponent's legs. He moves that leg back and kicks in turn. A high kick is permitted, and is caught with the hands. The object is to throw the opponent.

That Culin, a Western anthropologist, viewed taekyon as a game is significant, since he and the Western world as a whole at that time probably had little or no preconceptions of or categories for the Asian martial arts.

In addition, Lee Yong-bok, chairperson of the Traditional Taekyon Society and vice-chairperson of the Korea Taekyon Association in Seoul, notes that taekyon is often described in Korean dictionaries as "a contest in which two opponents try to knock each other down with a kick" (Lee, 1996). Pieter also notes that, in the *New World Korean-English Dictionary* (1979), taekyon is defined as a "kicking and tripping art (as a sport)" and the term *gakhui* (*gak-hi*) is a synonym for it (Pieter, 1994). It should be noted that no other Chinese, Japanese, or Korean martial art has ever been described as *hi* (*hei* in the Cantonese dialect of Chinese, *xi* in the pinyin system of romanization of the Mandarin dialect), with the exception of maybe certain forms of folk wrestling. The fact that both Culin, a Westerner, and the Koreans themselves called taekyon a game should suggest to us the nature of the art.

Learning and Playing

This game, due to its very nature and the nature of Korean society of the 1800s, was the exclusive domain of males. And as a game that was played out in the open (as the painting *Dae Kwai Do* shows[1]), at festivals and in the streets, it was probably played at one level or another by many of the boys and the young men and was not confined to those who learned it in a dojang setting. In fact, taekyon was probably not taught in a dojang until the Japanese prohibited it, forcing those who wished to practice it to do so secretly indoors or in remote locations. Before its prohibition by the authorities and as a game that was played in the streets or out in the open, many young Korean males learned many techniques in an intuitive and organic way, by watching, copying, and playing. That taekyon was also taught by master teachers to committed students before the Japanese takeover and prohibition is also a definite possibility, but most players probably learned it in a trial and error fashion out in the open. Those who learned by watching, copying, and playing probably learned some techniques here and there, but those privileged few who were committed enough to learn from master teachers were probably more able to learn the entire corpus of taekyon's techniques. Thus, men like Hwang Kee and Choi Hong-hi, considered the "founders" of tangsoodo and taekwondo, who claim to have learned some taekyon but do not have official records to back up their stories, may have actually learned some techniques of the art.

What Actually Happens During a Game of Taekyon?

In the beginning of the match, the two players stand with their feet apart, directly facing each other and bow to each other. After bowing, the players then move in synchronization with each other in and out of attack range with a rhythmic motion, swaying their arms up and down and from side to side, almost in a mirror image of each other. As the players move in sync with one another, they forcefully exhale air by making sounds ("eekeh" and "ekeh") in rhythm with their body motions in order to release ki. After one or more repetitions of this rhythmic motion, one of the players suddenly breaks the rhythm by launching an attack against the other player.

The object of the game is to down the opponent, and this can be done in several different ways. The simplest is just to knock the other player down with a kick. Although higher kicks to the torso and even to the head are allowed, the emphasis is on low-line kicking to the opponent's lower legs in order to knock out one of the legs, weaken the opponent's base of support, or to sweep the opponent off of his feet. Other ways to down an opponent include trapping or grabbing the kicking leg of the opponent with an arm and then throwing him with the other arm or sweeping his other leg with a kick. Taekyon also includes within its repertoire many techniques by which a player first unbalances his opponent by hooking one of the opponent's feet or legs and then proceeds to throw the opponent by a combined action of sweeping one of the opponent's legs with a kick and simultaneously pushing or pulling the opponent's upper body with a hand.

During the match, a player may move one leg to a position behind his body, in order to dodge the opponent's kicks and/or move his own leg to a better position to launch an attack. Otherwise, the players are standing directly in front of each other. The players may also jump into the air and kick with both legs. What are not allowed are any sort of hand or elbow strikes, attacks to the opponent's pressure points, or full-powered kicks.

TAEKYON KICKING PRACTICE

High kick to knock down the opponent.

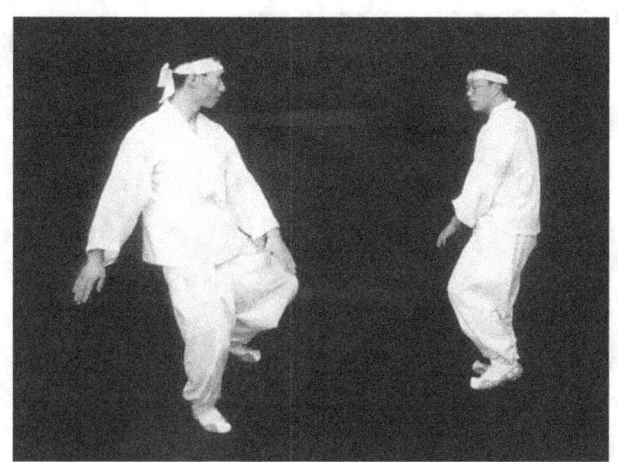

Left: Godenbaljil. Right: Deotgori.

Left: Ohgumchagi. Right: Nunjilochagi.

Lack of Philosophic Ideals

As a game that was played by young men, taekyon had none of the philosophic ideals that we now associate with the East Asian martial arts; it was simply a game. In his article, Young (1993) dismisses Hwang Kee's assertion that taekyon was looked down upon because it did not teach discipline and that it only contained non-specific offensive-defensive techniques. I believe there is much more than a grain of truth to this. Young (1993) mentions that Neo-Confucianism had "brought about a drastic decline of all martial arts practice outside the military," and the phrase "favoring the arts and despising arms" was the standard. Without Neo-Confucianism's support of the martial arts, from which moral or religious system can taekyon acquire its values?[2] Buddhism provided stimulus and patronage of the martial arts in East Asia of the past (e.g. Shaolin Temple monks, *sohei* warrior monks of Japan, Zen influence on the martial traditions of Japan) and still continues to do so. However, the ruling class of Korea during the Yi Dynasty (1392-1910) systematically sought to elevate Neo-Confucianism and denigrate Buddhism (Lee, 1976). Those who practiced taekyon did not teach Confucian values along with the art because they, along with most Koreans at that time, felt that the two were incompatible; to speak of Confucian values is to "despise arms." These practitioners could have related the art to Buddhist values, but due to the efforts of the ruling class, the teachings of Buddhism were also looked down upon.

Godochagi.

Other evidence that taekyon was looked down upon because it and those who practiced it lacked values such as discipline come from a passage in the *Haedong Chukki*, written in 1921 (Lee, 1990). This passage, written in classical Chinese, describes the object of a taekyon match and notes that there were three "methods":

> There is an old custom of a leg art, [where the persons] facing each other stand and kick each other down. There are three methods: The lowest is to kick the leg. The better one is to push the shoulder. Having the flying leg art is to kick down the topknot of the hair. In this way, [those who practiced the art] take revenge or gamble to fight for a beloved concubine. Since the courts prohibited it, now this game (*hi*) is no more. It is called taekyon.

Needless to say, what taekyon was used for and the fact that it was banned by the authorities point to its lack of moral value in the eyes of those in power.

Taekyon's parent art subak had also been banned during the Koryo Dynasty of the fourteenth century for similar reasons. Young (1993) notes that King Chung Mok outlawed it because onlookers were wagering so much money and property on subak matches. In Article 2 of the Punishments Section of the 39th Scroll of the *Koryo Saji* (*Historical Records of Koryo*), the text, written in classical Chinese, states that "As for *bak-hi* ('the game of subak'), those who gamble money or property each receives 100 paddle strikes, and [the game] is ended," i.e. prohibited (Lee, 1990). Taekyon and subak were definitely perceived to have a negative effect on the moral climate of society.

Taekyon's Criminal Connections

This brings us to taekyon's "criminal connection," which Hwang Kee (1970), founder of Moo Duk Kwan tangsoodo, mentions and Young (1993) dismisses as inconclusive. Given that taekyon lacked philosophic and moral values, its use by criminal elements should not come as a surprise. Other Korean martial artists have also mentioned that taekyon was practiced and used by street gangs before the Japanese occupation period. In a recent interview published in *Tae Kwon Do Times* (1997), Chung Do Kwan founder Lee Won-guk mentions that gangs of young males, in order to gain control of the streets, often fought each other using taekyon, and the government had to stop it.

This is also a common perception in the eyes of the Korean people, as illustrated in the film *The General's Son*, directed by Im Kwon-taek, one of Korea's most prolific and critically acclaimed directors. This movie is based on the true story of Kim Du-han, the son of a famous general who resisted the Japanese occupation of Korea from his base in Manchuria. As a child, Kim Du-han lived the life of a poor street kid in Seoul, away from his father, but through his fighting abilities, he got the attention of gang bosses and rose through the ranks of the gangs which controlled the streets of Seoul (as much as any Korean not working with the Japanese can control any place in Korea, given that the Japanese were in power). In the film, Kim became a local hero as he also defeated several Japanese martial artists in single combat. Eventually, Kim united the gangs of Seoul, and although not portrayed in this first film (there are at least two sequels), he became a well-known politician in his later years. Although his life was highly romanticized in the film, the situation of the times that the film sought to portray is quite accurate. The gangs were made up of toughs who extorted money from the merchants, but at least they resisted the Japanese and their running dogs, the much hated Koreans who were traitors to their own people. Gangs and the individuals who were members of those gangs rose to power not only through ruthlessness and street smarts, but also through force of arms. In other words, power came from knowing how to fight, and Kim Du-han fought well. And given that he was a street kid and a gangster, he probably did not have the privilege to learn Japanese martial arts but used the taekyon that he learned by watching, practicing, and testing it in fights in the streets.

There should be no stigma attached to taekyon's criminal connection. Many martial arts all over the world have such connections in their pasts, and they only make the understanding of the histories of those arts more interesting and colorful, and in no way are those arts looked down upon in modern times because once they were practiced by the less respected members of society. Examples abound: savate was partly developed by brawlers and ruffians who fought each other on the waterfronts of France's port cities;

capoeira was played by bandits, and those who practiced it were at the head of parading parties that fought each other when they met in the streets of some of the major cities of Brazil;[3] the Chinese martial arts were often practiced and used by secret societies and triad criminal elements; even Japanese jujutsu was looked down upon in the early Meiji period (1868-1912) because there were many who used it to bully others in a criminal fashion, to show off, or to prize fight, which of course paved the way for Jigoro Kano to create judo, a "do" form with philosophical ideals. Similarly, most modern Korean martial arts also have the "do" suffix, reflecting the effect that the Japanese concern for some of their martial arts to have philosophical underpinnings has had on the Korean understanding of what a martial art should be.

Modern Taekyon and Its Values

The term *taekyon* obviously does not have a "do" suffix and, as a folk art, it had no underlying philosophical ideals, as discussed above. That it was traditionally not practiced in a "dojang" is a natural conclusion, since a dojang is a place where the "do" (the "Way" of Confucianism, Daoism, and/or Buddhism) is cultivated, and taekyon had no such associations with those religions or philosophy systems. The usage of the term "dojang" to denote a place where the martial arts are studied came to Korea when the Japanese brought over the term "dojo." Both terms have the same meaning and are written with the same Chinese characters.

However, in its modern form, taekyon has acquired values from the above-mentioned philosophical systems. Lee Yong-bok (1996) writes that

"Throughout the years, Taekyon was carefully refined to fit in with the Korean lifestyles," and that if it did not fit in with such a "civilized" lifestyle, it would have been forgotten. Elsewhere, he describes in detail such Confucian values as courage, loyalty, filial piety, faithfulness, benevolence, ritual propriety, respect, and honesty that are Korean ideals and are now associated with taekyon. He also compares Korean martial values to those of Japanese bushido (Lee, 1990). Thus, taekyon's development in the twentieth century also mirrors what has happened with other Korean martial arts which have been extensively influenced by the Japanese understanding of the martial arts. Taekyon has also recently become a martial sport, continuing its development affected by Western sports theory.

Lineage, Cultural Purity, and Japanese Influence

The fact that modern taekyon lineage only goes back to several men who practiced it in the late nineteenth century (even though the art is much older) also points to the fact that it was very much a game (Young, 1993). In an open atmosphere, in which anyone can learn and play, no records needed to be kept. Why would anyone want to keep track of who learned from whom how to play a game that was looked down upon anyway? Such records of lineage were only kept when the art was forced underground and those who wished to preserve it kept a written record of those who learned its techniques in their schools. Such record keeping is counter-intuitive since if the Japanese had ever gotten hold of such records, the consequences would have been disastrous. But the record keeping was also necessary in order to keep the art alive, since now one can search out those who were actually formally instructed in taekyon.

Those who are concerned with the "cultural purity" (i.e., being unaffected by foreign influence—which has marked most modern Korean martial arts) of taekyon can also benefit from the understanding of the art as a folk game. When the Japanese martial arts were brought to Korea, those who brought them also brought the Japanese concern for lineage and legitimacy in the martial arts. Taekyon, as it was traditionally performed and played in the streets by the common people, probably had very little concern with lineage and legitimacy. Those who were able to learn formally from masters and had their names in records were probably few in number. The folk nature of taekyon points to its indigenousness.[4] Obsessiveness with legitimacy through lineage points to something that is foreign and desires exclusivity.

Traditionally, in addition to being a martial art, taekyon was a folk art and a game to be enjoyed and as a way to gain prestige, even though the skills acquired from its practice could be used to exact revenge, to fight for women, or to gain power and respect as a gangster. The playful aspect of taekyon and its resulting implications should not be overlooked or downplayed. In fact, I believe that looking at taekyon from this angle can open totally new vistas in our understanding of it. In our self-imposed and limited view of what an East Asian martial art should or should not be, we become neurotically obsessed with such issues as philosophy and lineage, and this blinds us to the fact that taekyon was simply considered a game and a folk art played by the common people.

Incorporating breathing
exercises into the taekyon regimen.

Since Robert Young's (1993) revelation of taekyon to the American martial arts community, there has been much building on to the foundation that he has laid, and our understanding of the nature and histories of the Korean martial arts has been greatly enriched. There is much controversy in this country as well as in Korea, over which martial arts are the legitimate heirs to the ancient Korean martial arts. As I reflect on the modern Korean martial arts, I believe that taekwondo and tangsoodo, along with modern taekyon, are in a very real sense the descendants of traditional taekyon. Not that I believe any of taekwondo's or tangsoodo's techniques actually came from taekyon,[5] but the emphasis on kicking definitely comes from taekyon and the Koreans' understanding of what their native martial arts are supposed to be like. Even as the Japanese martial arts flooded their country and taekyon waned, the Korean people did not forget that their native martial art emphasized leg maneuvers and that one had to be able to kick very well in order to fight the Korean way. This perception of the Korean martial arts has come down to this day as the Japanese arts were "Koreanized" to emphasize kicking techniques. However, modern taekyon, although rightfully the legitimate heir to the traditional Korean martial art, has also been "Japanized" to a certain extent now that it is very much concerned with lineage and philosophical ideals, and it has even been Westernized as it has become a sport.

Footnotes

[1] See Young (1993).

[2] It should be noted that the forms with which Neo-Confucianism manifested itself in the neighboring countries of China and Japan did not bring about the decline of martial arts in those countries. In fact, many of the values taught alongside the Chinese martial arts and those values of Japanese bushido come directly from Confucianism.

[3] There are many similarities between capoeira and taekyon and a detailed comparison may be warranted. In addition to the criminal element, both arts have the following in common:

1) Both arts have an emphasis on kicking.
2) Both arts, in certain forms, have triangular footwork (the Regional style of capoeira and taekyon as described by Steward Culin).
3) In the premodern era, both arts could be learned in an intuitive, trial-and-error manner as well as from master teachers (called "mestres" in capoeira).
4) In the modern era, both arts have been developed into competitive sports.
5) Both arts have dance-like qualities and can be performed accompanied by music and rhythm keepers.
6) Both arts are also games that were traditionally played out in the open while many people watched.

[4] Another folk aspect of taekyon which points to its indigenousness is its dance-like qualities which make it similar to and probably related to other traditional Korean folk dances. Taekyon players move with their bodies and swing their arms and legs to a rhythm "which beginning students sometimes learn while traditional Korean drums and bamboo flutes keep time" (Young,

1993). Although taekyon is descended from subak, which had come from China, its dance qualities make it unlike anything found in the Chinese martial arts (Young, 1993: 50; Lee, 1996: 50; Lee, 1990: 68).

[5] Burdick (1997) hints that modern taekyon (not traditional) may have influenced taekwondo with its circular kicking. Lee Yong-bok notes that taekyon "has traditionally emphasized stepping and stamping techniques directed at the opponent's lower legs and feet" and "focus[es] upon linear moves" (Young, 1993).

Bibliography

Burdick, D. (1997). People and events of taekwondo's formative years. *Journal of Asian Martial Arts*, 6: 1, pp. 30-49.

Capoeira, N. (1995). *The little capoeira book*. Berkeley, CA: North Atlantic Books.

Culin, S. (1895). *Korean games: With notes on the corresponding games of China and Japan*. Philadelphia: University of Philadelphia Press.

Hwang, K. (1970). *Su bak do dae gam*. Seoul, Korea: Han U Ri.

Lee, K. B. (1976). *A new history of Korea*. Cambridge, MA: Harvard University Press.

Lee, K. S. (March 1997). Grandmaster Won Kuk Lee: Founder of Chung Do Kwan (interview). *Tae Kwon Do Times*, pp. 44-51.

Lee, Y. B. (1990). Hanguk muyae taekkyon. Seoul, Korea: Hak Min Sa.

Lee, Y. B. (April 1996). Tracking tae-kyon: Tae-kyon, is it a dance or martial art? *Mudo Dojang*, pp. 50-53.

Pieter, W. (1994). Notes on the historical development of Korean martial sports: An addendum to Young's history and development of taekyon. *Journal of Asian Martial Arts*, 3: 1, pp. 82-89.

Young, R. (1993). The history and development of taekyon. *Journal of Asian Martial Arts*, 2: 2, pp. 44-69.

index

An, Ja-san, 18, 21
archery, 2-3, 11, 15, 18-19, 21, 42
broadsword, 4-5, 20
Buddhism, 2, 11, 13-16, 29-30, 39, 45, 53, 56
charioteering, 2, 42
Cheok Gye-gwang (see Qi Jiguang), 3-7, 20
Chongno dojang, 22, 37
Choi, Hong-hi, 13, 15-16, 18, 28-29, 49
Chosun Mu Sa Yeong Ung Jeon, 18, 21
Chosun Sang Go Sa, 21
Chosun Wang Jo Shil Lok, 19
Chun, Richard, 13
Chung Do Kwan, 55
Chung, Kyeong-hwa, 19, 24, 28, 34-35, 37
Confucianism, 2, 20-21, 45, 52-53, 56, 59
criminal element, 21, 55-56, 59 note 3
Dae Kwai Do painting, 10, 18-19, 27, 49
double-edged straight sword, 8
elite guards, 3
firearms/guns, 4, 20
guardian, 2, 13-14, 16
Gurigae dojang, 19, 22, 37
halberd, 4, 20
Han, Il-dong, 28
hapkido, 25, 29-31
Harmon, Barry, 29
History of the Three Kingdoms (Samguk Sagi), 40-41, 45
Hong, Mong-hwa, 21
Huang, Chang-rang, 5, 7
Hwang, Kee, 12, 16, 21, 25-27, 29
hwarang, 2, 7, 14-15, 25, 30-31, 39-45
Hyesan, Yusu, 10, 19
Illustrated Encyclopedia of Martial Arts Manuals (Muye Dobo Tongji), 2-3, 6-7, 20, 39
Im, Ho, 22-23, 37
jujutsu, 5, 7, 11, 31, 56

karate, 6-7, 8 note 4, 18, 26-29, 31, 43
Kim, Du-han, 55
Kim, Gu, 22
Kim, Hong-do, 18
Kim, Hong-shik, 19, 22-23, 37
Kim, Il-nam, 29-30
Kim, Mu-jin, 31
Kim, Pu-sik, 40
Kim, Soo, 28
King Chinhung, 41, 45
King Jongjo, 4, 7
King Kojong, 21
King Pophung, 41
Korea Athletic Association, 26
Korea Hapkido Association, 29
Korea Kuk Sool Association, 25
Korean Kuk Sool-Hapkido Association, 25
Korea Tang Soo Do Association, 26
Korea Traditional Taekyon National Headquarters, 24
Korea Traditional Taekyon Research Association, 19, 24
Korean Kuk Sool-Hapkido Association, 25
Korean Soo Bahk Do Association, 26
Korea Taekyon Association, 48
Korea Yoo Sool Association, 31
kuksul, 25-26, 29-31
Kuk Sool Won, 29
Kumkang Yuksa, 16, 27
Lee, Joo-bang, 29-30
Lee, Won-guk, 55
Lee, Yong-bok, 15-16, 19, 22-24, 28, 33, 35-37, 48, 56, 60
Man Mul Bo, 18
Manchuria, 12, 21, 25-27, 55
masked sword dance, 6
Memories of the Three Kingdoms (Samguk

Yusa), 7, 30, 40-41, 45
Mongolia, 10-11
Moo Duk Kwan, 26, 55
Neo-Confucianism, 20-21, 52-53, 59 note 2
New Book of Effective Discipline, 4
Pak, Man-yup, 34-35, 37
Pak, Mu-gyeong, 22, 37
Pak, Tul-baek, 22, 37
pressure-point, 17, 30-31, 36
Qi, Jiguang, 3-7, 20
Records of the Hwarang (Hwarang Segi), 30
Rhee, Syngman, 23
sabre, 20
Seo, In-sun, 11, 25, 27, 29
Shi, Chae-ho, 12, 21
Shin, Han-seung, 19, 22-24, 32, 36-37
Shin, Jae-young, 22-23, 37
ssirum, 10, 18-19
Sohn, Tae-soo, 26
Song Duk-ki, 19-20, 22-23, 31-32, 37
spear, 3-5, 13, 15-16, 19-20
Suahm Dosa, 30
subakdo, 12, 21, 25-27, 44
Subakdo Dae Gam, 12
sword practice, 2-3, 5, 8 notes 1 and 2, 13-15
Tae Jong Shil Lok, 18
taekwondo, 6-7, 8 note 4, 13, 16, 25, 27-29, 31-33, 39-40, 43-44, 49, 58
Taekwon-do: the Korean Art of Self-Defence, 28
taekyon, 5, 12, 18-19, 37 note, 47-48
tangsoodo, 6-6, 8 note 4, 12, 21, 25-27, 43-44, 49, 55, 58
thirty-two boxing forms, 4-5
Thomas, Chris, 27, 29
Traditional Taekyon Society, 48
trident, 4, 20
Veritable Records of the Yi Dynasty, 2-3
Wangshimni dojang, 22, 37
Won Gwang, 15, 30, 445
World Kuksool Association, 29
World War II, 11, 23, 28-29, 40

wrestling, 1-3, 6, 11, 18-19, 24, 28
Yi, Dok-Mu, 4-5, 7
Yi, Seong-ji, 18
yudo, 25
yusul, 11, 17-18, 25, 31